D0622900

The Old Man Who Does As He Pleases
Selections from the Poetry and Prose of Lu Yu

Prepared for the Columbia College Program of Translations from the Oriental Classics

The Old Man Who Does As He Pleases

Selections from the Poetry and Prose
of Lu Yu

Translated by Burton Watson

Columbia University Press
New York and London 1973

Burton Watson, Professor of Chinese at Columbia University, is the author of *Ssu-ma Ch'ien, Grand Historian of China* (1958), *Early Chinese Literature* (1962), and *Chinese Lyricism:* Shih *Poetry from the Second to the Twelfth Century* (1971) and the translator of *Records of the Grand Historian of China, translated from the* Shih chi *of Ssu-ma Ch'ien*, 2 vols. (1961), *Su Tung-p'o: Selections from a Sung Dynasty Poet* (1965), *Basic Writings of Mo Tzu, Hsün Tzu, and Han Fei Tzu* (1967), *The Complete Works of Chuang Tzu* (1968), *Cold Mountain: 100 Poems by the T'ang Poet Han-shan* (reissue, 1970), and *Chinese Rhyme-Prose: Poems in the Fu Form from the Han and Six Dynasties Periods* (1971).

Library of Congress Cataloging in Publication Data

Lu, Yu, 1125–1210.
   The old man who does as he pleases.

   I. Watson, Burton, 1925–   tr.   II. Title.
PL2687.L8A28   895.1′1′4   73-10278
ISBN 0-231-03766-X

For Elisabeth Shoemaker
with many thanks for
the twelve preceding books as well

Contents

Introduction

Scholars have traditionally looked upon the T'ang dynasty (618–907) as the great age of Chinese poetry, when elegance of diction and depth of sensitivity combined to produce verses that are miracles of concision and evocative power. Beside its golden treasures, the poetic works of the succeeding Sung dynasty (960–1280) have seemed to native critics to be made of drabber stuff, less pure in distillation, more diffuse and low-keyed in outlook. In recent years, however, there has been a movement to reexamine these assumptions and, while not challenging the greatness of T'ang poetry, to discern in the works that followed it new values and sources of interest. Particularly among Western readers, Sung poetry has begun to be prized precisely because of its startling range of subject, its philosophical complexity, its unfastidious realism and colloquial turns of phrase, qualities that in the past might have been looked upon as faults, but which in many ways ally it with current trends in Western poetry. In an earlier volume in this series I set out to introduce to the English reader some of the representative works of Su Tung-p'o, the leading poet of the era known as the Northern Sung (960–1126). The present volume is an attempt to do the same for the most important poet of the era that succeeded it, the Southern Sung (1127–1280), presenting selections from the poetry and prose of Lu Yu, better known in the Far East by his literary name Fang-weng, or "The Old Man Who Does As He Pleases."

Lu Yu was born in 1125 in the midst of a violent rain storm as his father, an official in the Northern Sung government, was traveling along the Huai River by boat with his wife and family on the way to a new assignment. A few months later, the

Jurchen, a non-Chinese people of Manchuria who had established a state called the Chin on the Sung's northern border, marched south into China. The following year the Sung capital at Pien-ching (present-day K'ai-feng) fell to the invaders and most of the court fled south. In 1127 a new emperor came to the throne, eventually establishing his capital at Hangchow in Chekiang, and the era known as the Southern Sung began. Though attempts were made to drive back the Chin armies, in time a peace treaty was signed whereby the Sung recognized Chin sovereignty over the old heartland of China, the area north of the Huai River, and agreed to pay a yearly tribute in silver and silk.

Lu Yu's father belonged to a highly vocal and uncompromising group of officials who adamantly opposed the humiliation of such a settlement and repeatedly called for military action to expel the invaders and recover control of the north. Lu Yu passionately endorsed his father's views, in his poetry expressing his indignation at the shame his nation was forced to suffer, his pity for his captive countrymen in the north, and his impatience for the day of vengeance. Though one cannot question the sincerity and ardor of his pleas, he and the others who shared his views do not seem to have been very well informed about the true situation in the north, and consistently underestimated the difficulties of a strike against the Chin. The only attempt at such a military action came late in Lu Yu's life, in 1206–7, and ended in signal failure. Lu Yu died in 1210 without ever seeing his dream of a united China brought to fulfillment.

When the north fell to the Chin armies, Lu Yu's father fled with his family to his home in Shao-hsing in Chekiang, southeast of Hangchow, where Lu Yu grew up and began preparing himself for an official career. But, because he and his father belonged to the group advocating war, while the government was dominated by the party of peace and conciliation, he failed to achieve any appreciable success in the world of officialdom. He flunked the civil service examination three times, the last time because his enemies in the government insisted that his "pass" be changed to a "fail." He held a series of rather insignificant posts in eastern China, and later in the area of Szechwan in the west, but was four times dismissed from office, ostensibly because of drunkenness and inattention to duty, though probably in fact because his hawkish views offended those in power. His later years were largely spent in retirement at his home in the countryside in Shao-hsing, where he received a meager pension from the government in recognition of his years of official service and his eminence as a man of letters, and worked along with his sons at a life of farming. Though, like all Chinese writers, he began at an early age to lament his gray hair and failing powers, he surprised himself and others by living to the age of eighty-four—by Chinese reckoning, eighty-five, since a child is regarded as one year old at the time of birth—thus becoming one of the longest lived of Chinese poets.

He was also one of the most prolific, leaving behind a collection of close to ten thousand poems, as well as miscellaneous prose writings. Most of his extant poems were written after the age of forty. His youthful works, probably cast in the difficult and allusive style associated with the Chiang-hsi School, apparently displeased him and were largely suppressed when, at the age of sixty-five, he prepared a collection of his poems in twenty chapters. This collection, known as the *Chien-nan shih-kao* (hereafter abbreviated as CNSK), was twice added to by one of his sons who, out of motives of filial piety, no doubt strove for comprehensiveness rather than selectivity, until in 1220, eleven years after the poet's death, it reached the eighty-five chapter form in which it has come down to us today. The poems are arranged chronologically, and thus constitute a biography of the poet's mature years.

Lu Yu is a poet of many moods and styles, but it is generally agreed that two themes dominate his writings. One is that of patriotic indignation, his longing to see the north, which he was too young even to remember, once more restored to native rule, a longing that often appears in his poetry in the form of fitful dreams in which he sees himself and his countrymen actually riding into battle against the hated barbarians. The other theme, wholly different in nature, is that of the quiet joys and experiences of everyday life. Lu Yu made no secret of his extreme fondness for wine, and in 1176, after being dismissed from a post on charges of "drunkenness and irresponsibility," he adopted in a gesture of defiance the literary name Fang-weng, which means "the old man who does as he pleases." In countless poems, particularly those written late in life, when he was living in retirement in Shao-hsing, it is this theme of carefree enjoyment of life that predominates. In the former type of poetry, in which Lu Yu appears as an ardent activist, patriot, and reformer, he clearly identifies himself with the great T'ang poet Tu Fu (712–70), whose works he admired intensely. The other Lu Yu, the contented, philosophical farmer, derives eventually from another great poet of the past, T'ao Yüan-ming or T'ao Ch'ien (365–427), who was likewise one of Lu Yu's literary idols.

The central problem in the interpretation of Lu Yu's life and works is that of how these two disparate themes and facets of personality are related within a single man. It is no question of youthful ardor followed by the mellowness of old age, for both themes appear side by side from the poet's earliest extant works to those of his final year. We are dealing here with no simple linear development, but a much more complex amalgam of elements in the poet's makeup that made him yearn for an opportunity to come to the aid of his country at the same time that his uncompromising bluntness and disdain for convention rendered his advancement in political life all but impossible; that kept him dreaming of war banners and battle charges at the very moment he seemed most resigned to the quiet life and its simple pleasures. No one to my knowledge has offered a satisfactory solution to these contradictions in his character —I mention the problem here only to prepare the reader for the startling alternation of moods which he will encounter in my selection.

Lu Yu wrote many works in the *ku-shih* or "old poetry" form, which observes no restrictions in length and does not make use of tonal parallelism. But, like Tu Fu, he had a great fondness for the so-called modern style forms, with their much more complex technical requirements. He particularly excelled in the *lü-shih* or regulated verse form, an eight-line form that observes elaborate rules of tonal parallelism and requires strict verbal parallelism in the two middle couplets of the poem. Lu Yu's adroit handling of verbal parallelism in these poems in *lü-shih* form has been particularly admired by later readers and, I hope, will be apparent even in English translation. In addition, he wrote often in the *chüeh-chü* form which, like the *lü-shih*, observes rules of tonal parallelism but is restricted to four lines in length. In my translations I have indicated the number of characters in the line and the form of the original so that the reader may readily identify these various forms.

Faced with such a staggering volume of poetry, one obviously may, by his manner of selection, create any number of different images of the poet. In the sixty-three poems that follow, I have no doubt created a Lu Yu of my own, though this was done less on the basis of any preconceived idea of Lu Yu's true worth and identity than on that of what poems I thought would go well into English. For the reader's information, however, it may be well to say a few words about my own reactions to his poetry and the problems involved in translating it into English.

Like many modern readers, I find Lu Yu's constant calls to battle, no matter how sincere in conviction and noble in final objective, rather difficult to sympathize with, though I have made a conscious effort to overcome my prejudices in this respect. Personal feelings aside, his patriotic poems seem to me difficult to translate precisely because of their intensely personal and passionate nature which, if not brought over into just the right language, is likely to sound petulant and bombastic. I have tried to include enough examples of his patriotic poetry to give the reader an idea of what it is like, though I am conscious that I have probably done less than justice to this aspect of his work.

Much more to my taste are the poems of everyday life, particularly the life of the farming village, not because of any great philosophical depth or insight they possess—other poets of the rustic life such as T'ao Yüan-ming are more interesting in this respect—but for their amazing wealth and precision of detail. Earlier poets had tended to be fairly conventional in their choice of detail, and certain stock images of village life—the barking dogs, the roosting chickens—had been employed century after century with only minor variation to evoke the landscape and mood of the countryside. Lu Yu, however, like the other great Sung poets, was not content with a mere manipulation of the images inherited from the literature of the past, but ceaselessly worked to fill his poems with all the actual sights, sounds, and smells of the village around him. His rustic poems, notwithstanding the great number and rapidity in which they were produced and their relative absence of impassioned feeling, have a kind of reportorial vividness and homey realism that make them consistently engrossing. It is these poems of daily life, with their abundance of succinct and evocative detail, that have won the admiration of readers in China and, introduced to Japan in late Tokugawa times, influenced the development of the haiku form. They are also the poems which, in my opinion, go best into English and are most likely to appeal to the modern reader, and I have accordingly made them the core of my selection. Particularly to be prized are those poems of his closing years in which, with a vigor and acuity that belie his advanced age, he calls into being the scenes of his youth. Few works of literature so magnificently attest the power of the imagination to transcend the incursions of time and senescence as do these poems of Lu Yu's last years.

Among Lu Yu's prose writings, the work of most interest to the general reader is undoubtedly his famous *Ju-Shu-chi* or "Diary of a Trip to Shu." Late in the fifth year of the *ch'ien-tao* era (1169), the poet received word that he had been appointed to the post of *t'ung-p'an* or vice-governor of the province of K'uei-chou. The city of K'uei-chou, where the administrative offices were situated, was on the Yangtze River just west of the gorges, in the region called Shu, which corresponds to present-day Szechwan Province. Because of illness, Lu Yu did not set off for his new post immediately. It was the summer of the following year, 1170, before he left his home in Shao-hsing and journeyed by boat north on the Grand Canal to the Yangtze and then westward upriver to K'uei-chou. He kept a diary of the journey, the *Ju-Shu-chi*, beginning with the fifteenth day of the fifth intercalary month and continuing with almost daily entries until the time when he reached his destination on the twenty-seventh day of the tenth month, a period of 156 days. In it he describes the sights along the canal and the river, the people he encountered, the temples, shrines, and scenic spots he visited, and the harrowing experiences of a passage through the Yangtze gorges. Simple and direct, with relatively little literary embellishment or philosophical musing, his narrative is valuable both for the detailed and vivid picture it presents of life in central China in the twelfth century, and for the light it sheds on the personality of the poet.

My translation of excerpts from the diary represents approximately one third of the original. I have tried to concentrate on the journey itself, and have therefore omitted a number of entries that are concerned with side trips the poet took when the boat was under repair or could not proceed because of adverse winds, though many of these passages, such as that describing a visit to the Buddhist temples of Mount Lu, are of considerable interest in their own right. I have also made cuts here and there in some of the translated entries, usually in places where Lu Yu disgresses on the history of the place he is visiting or quotes lines from earlier poets who wrote about it. Likewise omitted in most cases are the lists of local officials whom the poet met in the course of his journey. Though my translation is incomplete, I hope it will suggest something of the great variety of material found in the diary and the breadth of the poet's interests.

Translator's Note

In preparing the translations of the poems I have consulted with profit the Japanese translations of selected poems by Suzuki Torao (*Riku Hōō shikai*, 3 vols., Tokyo, 1950); Ikkai Tomoyoshi (*Riku Yū*, Chūgoku shijin senshū 2d series #8, Iwanami, 1962); Maeno Naoaki (*Riku Yū*, Kanshi taikei series #19, Tokyo, 1964), and seventeen poems translated by Yang Hsien-yi and Gladys Yang which were published in *Chinese Literature* 8/1963, pp. 72–79, Foreign Languages Press, Peking. A volume of English translations from the poetry of Lu Yu entitled *The Rapier of Lu: Patriot Poet of China*, Clara Candlin (London: J. Murray, Wisdom of the East series), appeared in 1946. A few of my translations have appeared earlier in Yoshikawa Kojiro, *An Introduction to Sung Poetry* (Cambridge, Mass.: Harvard University Press, 1967), and my *Chinese Lyricism: Shih Poetry from the Second to the Twelfth Century* (New York: Columbia University Press, 1971), which works the reader may wish to consult for further information on Sung poetry.

To the best of my knowledge, no competently annotated version of the *Ju-Shu-chi* has yet been published, though one is very much needed. I have consulted the *Nyū Shokki chūshaku* of Ōtsuki Tōyō (Tokyo, 1881); the excerpt from the diary (ch. 6) in the *Lu Yu hsüan-chi* of Chu Tung-jun (Shanghai, 1962); and the Japanese translation by Yonaiyama Tsuneo (*Nyū Shokki*, Tokyo, 1944), though the annotation in all of these is highly inadequate and the last contains numerous errors. My translation, based on the text found in volume 1 of the *Lu Fang-weng ch'üan-chi*, Chung-kuo wen-hsüeh ming-chu ti-chi, Yang Chia-lo ed. (Taipei, 1963), is tentative at many points and I can only hope that scholars more versed in the geography and life of the period will be kind enough to point out my errors.

I wish to express my thanks to Professor Ogawa Tamaki of Kyoto University for calling these works on the *Ju-Shu-chi* to my attention and assisting me in the preparation of the translation of excerpts from the diary, though he is in no way responsible for its shortcomings.

The Old Man Who Does As He Pleases

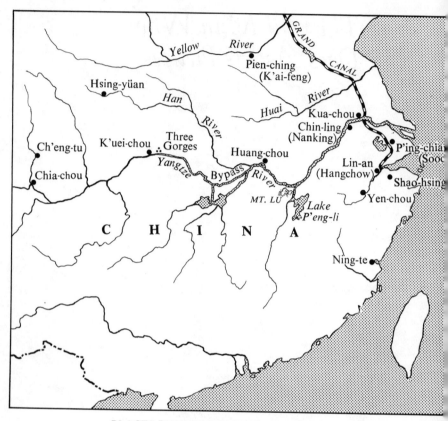

PLACES IMPORTANT IN THE LIFE OF LU YU

Crossing the Floating Bridge
to Get to South Terrace

(Written in 1159, when Lu Yu was an official at Ning-te in Fu-chou, present Fukien Province. South Terrace was the name of the river, but here refers to the hills along the riverbank. The bridge, made of planks laid across rows of boats, was wide enough for nine carriages to go abreast. The poet, thirty-five, was already talking about his gray hairs. 7-ch. *lü-shih;* CNSK 1.)

A stranger here, sick a lot, neglecting the sights;
all this talk I've heard of South Terrace—why not try a
    trip?
Nine wheeltracks stately stretching over the angry waves;
1,000 boats strung together right across the great river's heart!
Temple towers: bell and drum hurrying the twilight and
    dawn;
villages: banked in mist, now as in time gone by.
White hairs have no power to dampen the heroic mood I'm in;
drunk, I blow on a transverse flute, sitting in the banyan's
    shade.

Seeing Brother Seven Off to Military Headquarters at Yang-chou

(1162; Brother Seven means he was seventh in age among Lu Yu's brothers and male cousins of the same surname; Yang-chou was an important city north of the Yangtze in Kiangsu. The first six lines refer to events of the previous year, when Chin forces marched south as far as Kua-chou on the north bank of the Yangtze, not far from Shih-t'ou or Nanking, where the poet held office. Later in the year the invaders were defeated and withdrew to the region of Huai-nan north of Yang-chou. 7-ch. *lü-shih*; CNSK 1.)

First, reports of border beacons flashing word to Shih-t'ou;
in no time we heard barbarian horsemen were massing at
     Kua-chou.
Who among their Lordships would listen to a woodcutter's
     plan?
You and I helplessly fretting, like worried peasants in the
     field,
Swift snow battered the window—our hearts too were
     dashed and broken;
from steep towers we scanned the distance, my tears paired
     with yours.
How could I have known, on the Huai-nan road today,
in whirling catkins, flying petals, I'd be seeing you off by
     boat?

A Trip to Mountain West Village

(1167, when the poet was living at a place called Three Mountains in Shao-hsing in Chekiang. The "muddy" wine is milky unrefined rice wine, made in the last month of the year. 7-ch. *lü-shih;* CNSK 1.)

Don't laugh because it's muddy—year-end wine brewed in
    country homes;
harvests were good—to make the guest linger, fowl and
    pork aplenty.
Mountains multiply, streams double back—I doubt there's
    even a road;
willows cluster darkly, blossoms shine—another village
    ahead!
Pipe and drum sounds tagging me—spring festival soon;
robe, cap of plain and simple cut—they honor old ways
    here.
From now on, if I may, when time and moonlight allow,
I'll take my stick and, uninvited, come knock at your evening
    gate.

In the Rain Tying Up at Chao Village
I Was Moved to Write This

(1170, traveling up the Yangtze by boat on the way to a post at
K'uei-chou in Szechwan; see the poet's diary of the trip, p. 89. 7–
ch. *lü-shih*; CNSK 2.)

Homing swallows, swans on their way—both down my
    spirits;
reed blossoms, maple leaves—tying up at a lonely village.
Wind whips the dark waves—we put out more mooring
    lines;
rain brings a new cold—half the houses have shut their
    doors.
From the fish market, cooking smoke trails bleak across the
    sky;
at the dragon shrine, pipes and drums shrill in the yellow dusk.
Just so I stay well, nothing else to fret over!
Ahead may be hard roads, but that's not worth a mention.

Drunk Song

(1170, on the same journey, traveling through Hupei. The region was the site of the ancient kingdom of Ch'u, and Lu Yu has in mind the sad downfall of the state in the third century B.C. 7-ch. *ku-shih*; CNSK 2.)

Old boatman unsteps the mast, brakes it against green rocks;
drops of water pock the sandy shore, foot after foot of stains.
Autumn's gone but here by the Yangtze no foliage withers or
falls;
oak leaves are thick and shiny, maple leaves red.
Men of Ch'u from times past have had many sorrows;
even now, songs they sing walking the road bring a twinge of
pain.
Wild flowers blue and purple—gather them by the fistful;
valley fruit green and red—now just right for picking.
On the way I found some wine, watery but still not bad;
at river's edge, getting drunk as I please, no regret in the
world.
A thousand years of history's ups and downs here before my
eyes;
this great bustling border, the river, soaked in evening hues.
A hungry swan, wings drooping, skims over the boat;
in its heart it too must feel the same sadness as I.
Three times I thump the gunwale, can't shake this depression
off!
The moon brightens—now it shines on my crooked crow-
black hat.

Blue Rapids

(1170, ascending the Three Gorges of the Yangtze; the drumming
noise made with the oars signaled the departure of the boat. 7-ch.
ku-shih; CNSK 2.)

A hundred men shouting at once, helping to rattle the oars;
in the boat, face to face, we can't even hear ourselves talk.
All at once the men have scattered—silence, no more scuffle;
the only sound, two winches reeling out hundred-yard tow-
     lines:
whoo-whoo, whaa-whaa—how fast the winches unwind,
boatmen already standing there on the sandy shore!
Fog lifts from reedy villages, red in the setting sun;
rain ended, from fishermen's huts the damp smoke of cooking
     fires.
I turn my head, look toward home, now a thousand mountains
     away;
a trip up the gorges—we've just passed rapids number one.
When I was young I used to dream of the joys of official
     travel;
older now, I know just how hard the going can be.

At Ta-an I got sick from wine and
had to lay over for half a day.
Governor Wang invited me to his
place again but I didn't go,
so he sent me some wine to help me
get over my hangover. Accordingly,
I drank a little at River Moon Inn

(1172, on the way to Hsing-yüan in Shensi. 7-ch. *chüeh-chü;*
CNSK 3.)

River inn spring hangover—half a day's delay,
plus troubling the governor to send over wine so I could clear
     my head.
Masses and masses of willow flowers on the banks of the Chia-
     ling;
something special—at sky's end, today's case of the dumps!

Long Sigh: Written When Spending the Night at Green Mountain Store

(1172, traveling on official business through the Szechwan mountains. 5-ch. *ku-shih;* CNSK 3.)

One long sigh piled on another;
my travels never come to an end!
Ice and frost harry the dying year;
bird and beast cry in the sinking sun.
Sound of autumn fulling mallets fills the lonely village;
dead leaves bury the run-down inn.
White headed, I faced a ten thousand-mile road—
to fall into this lair of leopards and tigers.
By the roadside, marks of a fresh kill:
grease and blood stains on the bushes and thorns.
Always I've aimed for a heart of steel and stone,
forgetting family, to think of duty to my country;
but here in this place of nine parts death,
my dying would be no help to either family or state.
The heartland so long lost to invaders,
a man of spirit must drown his chest in tears.
Don't despise me for a bookish scholar—
a horse under me, I could strike the foe!

Running into Light Rain on
the Road to Sword Gate Pass

(1172, on the way to a post in Szechwan. In the last two lines Lu Yu is thinking of how Li Po and other famous T'ang poets were said to have composed verses while jogging along on donkeyback, and implying that, like his idol Tu Fu, he would far rather be a maker of government policy than of verse. 7-ch. *chüeh-chü*; CNSK 3.)

On my clothes the dust of travel mingled with wine stains;
a distant journey—no place that doesn't jar the soul!
And I—am I really meant to be a poet?
In fine rain straddling a donkey I enter Sword Gate Pass.

Third Month, Night of the Seventeenth, Written while Drunk

(1173, in Szechwan. 7-ch. *ku-shih;* CNSK 3.)

Years ago feasting on raw whale by the eastern sea,
white waves like mountains flinging me their beauty and awe;
last year shooting tigers, south mountain autumn,
coming home at night, thick snow plastered on my sable coat;
this year—so worn and broken it really makes you laugh;
hair flecked gray, ashen face—ashamed to look at myself!
Who'd think, given some wine, I could still raise a fuss,
yanking off my cap, facing men, a big shout for every one?
Traitorous barbarians still not crushed, my heart never at
    peace;
the lone sword by my pillow sings out its clanging cry.
In a fallen-down post-house I wake from dreams, the lamp
    about to go out;
tapping at the window, wind and rain—third watch by
    now.

After Getting Drunk, I Scribble Songs and Poems in Grass Script — Written as a Joke

(1173, at a post in Chia-chou in Szechwan; the "vermilion tower" is the government office. 7-ch. *ku-shih;* CNSK 4.)

Head poking from a vermilion tower, all eight directions
      cramped;
one dip of green wine and I go on for a hundred cups,
washing away the humps and hills, cliffs and crags of my
      heart,
cleansing myself so I can shape verses passionate, windy and
      free.
Ink at first spurts out like the ire of demons and gods;
characters all at once grow lean, formed like fallen dragons;
now a rare sword, drawn from its sheath, flashes a snowy
      blade;
now a great ship, cleaving the waves, speeds its gusty mast.
Paper gone, I fling down the brush with a lightning-and-thun-
      der crash;
womenfolk flee in astonishment, little boys run and hide.
Once I drafted a proclamation to chide the western realm;
whirr, whirr, the sound of my brush stirred in the hall of
      state.[1]

1. A reference to the time when, on behalf of the prime minister the poet drafted a dispatch to be sent to the Hsi-hsia state of Central Asia.

Then one day I turned my steps from court and suddenly ten
      years passed;
west I skimmed over the Three Pa, to the far end of Yeh-lang.
Mountains and rivers remote and wild, their customs strange;
luckily there's fine wine, the kind to put me in a trance.
In the midst of drunkenness I pull the cap from my head;
I permit no trace of frost to invade this green-black hair.
Gains and losses of a man's life—truly a piddling matter;
who says old age is so full of sorrow and woe?

With Ho Yüan-li Admiring Lotus Flowers, I Thought Back to the Old Outings at Mirror Lake

(1174, in Szechwan. On Mirror Lake at the poet's old home in
Shao-hsing, see p. 45. The rainbow breath in line one is an
indication of the poet's high spirits. 7-ch. *ku-shih*; CNSK 5.)

In wild youth wine was a joke, breath coming out in rain-
        bows;
one laugh hardly over, I'd drained a thousand cups.
In breezy halls we lowered the blinds—the girls were like
        jade;
moonbeams cool and clear filtered through speckled bamboo.
At third watch in painted boats we wound among the flowers,
flowers our four walls, boats for our home.
No need to go treading roots of the lotus—[1]
a mere whiff of flower scent, already the wine was gone.
So deep in flowers you couldn't see the painted boats moving,
just the sound of people singing "White Homespun," empty
        on the wind from the sky.
Paired paddles headed home, toying with lake waters;
here and there around the lakeside, people already out of bed.
And now I'm lean and shriveled, not worth a mention,
only lucky to have Mr. Ho to share this cask of wine.
The pink and green a bit scarce, but don't complain—
last year at Chia-chou, no lotuses at all to look at!

1. A reference to the line by Tu Fu: "Treading lotus roots in the
mud of the field," from the poem entitled "Accompanying Lord
Yen Cheng on a Sightseeing Trip to North Pond" written in 764.

On a Painting of Horses by Lung-mien

(1174, in Szechwan. Lung-mien, "The Layman of Lung-mien Mountain," is another name for Li Kung-lin [b. 1049], a painter of Northern Sung times. 7-ch. *ku-shih;* CNSK 5.)

Since our nation lost the western borderlands,
year after year we buy horses from these southwest tribes;
bred in feverish pastures, no stamina, no style,
yet at year's end to the frontier come how many hides in pay?
All knobs and angles, thin-boned, scarred with official brands,
lined up, they look as though they couldn't stand against a
    breeze.
Keeper of the Stable, Grand Coachman—why hand out
    these empty titles?
Dragon-match, blood-sweater—when will they come
    again? [1]
Painter Li in a time of peace held office in the capital;
a palace guard, many times he must have seen the steeds of
    Wo-wa.[2]
This fine silk frayed with the years, ink colors gone dark,
but the spirit of champions remains, never to be bridled!
To praise the heroic, love the old—a taste some men have;
troubled by events, fearful for my country, in vain I go on
    grieving.
Ah—where can I find three thousand horses coated and
    boned like these?

1. Dragon-match and blood-sweater were famous horses or
breeds of horses in ancient times.

2. A river in Kansu in a region famous for fine horses.

Riders gagged for sudden attack, I'd lead them in the night
  across the rocks of Sang-kan! [3]

3. The Sang-kan River flows south of Peking, where the Chin
had its capital at this time.

Eating Shepherd's Purse

(1176, in Szechwan. Third in a series of three; 7-ch. *chüeh-chü*; CNSK 7.)

A little dab of salt and pickled mincemeat
    to help bring out the flavor;
a touch of ginger and cinnamon
    to pick my spirits up;
on a clay stove, in a pot from Sheh,
    the poor family's salvation—
this wonderful secret—do I dare reveal it to the world?

Border Mountain Moon

(1177; vermilion gates in line three refers to the mansions of the nobles and high officials; the kettles mentioned in line five were pounded at night in army camps to signal the hour. 7-ch. *ku-shih* in *yüeh-fu* or ballad style; CNSK 8.)

Fifteen years ago the edict came: peace with the invader;
our generals fight no more but idly guard the border.
Vermilion gates still and silent; inside they sing and dance;
stabled horses fatten and die, bows come unstrung.
From garrison towers the beat of kettles hurries the sinking
    moon;
lads who joined the troops at twenty, white-haired now.
In the sound of the flutes who will read the brave man's heart?
Above the sands emptily shining, moon on warrior bones.
Spear-clash on the central plain—this we've known from
    old.
But when have traitorous barbarians lived to see their heirs?
Our captive people, forbearing death, pine for release,
even tonight how many places stained with their tears?

River Tower

(1177, in Szechwan; the previous year, the poet had been dismissed from his post on charges of "drunkenness and irresponsibility." Paper-making was an important industry in the area. 5-ch. *lü-shih;* CNSK 8.)

Heavy rain washed away the last of the mugginess;
at river's edge quietly I lean from a tower.
The sun sits on the level fields, sinking;
water purls around a broken raft, flowing on.
Pounding paper—evening in a tumbledown village;
calling the cows—autumn in the narrow old lanes.
Stale pedant with his worries for the state—
at this point all he does is scratch his head.

Idle Thoughts

(1177, at Ch'eng-tu in Szechwan. 7-ch. *lü-shih;* CNSK 9.)

Thatch gate works all right but I never open it,
afraid people walking might scuff the green moss.
Fine days bit by bit convince me spring's on the way;
fair winds come now and then, wrapped up with market
    sounds.
Studying the Classics, my wife asks about words she doesn't
    know,
tasting the wine, my son pours till the cup overflows.
If only I could get a little garden, half an acre wide—
I'd have yellow plums and green damsons growing all at once!

At Lung-hsing Temple, Paying Sad Respects at the Place Where Master Shao-ling Stayed for a Time

(1178, on the Yangtze at Chung-chou in Szechwan. Master Shao-ling is the T'ang poet and official Tu Fu, who stayed at the temple for a time in the autumn of 765. The first two lines refer to the rebel leader An Lu-shan and his soldiers, many of them non-Chinese, who captured the two T'ang capitals at Lo-yang and Ch'ang-an and forced the emperor and his court to flee. The parallel with Lu Yu's own age is obvious. 7-ch. *chüeh-chü*; CNSK 10.)

Heartland in strife and turmoil,
  robbed of its age-long peace,
battle fires, barbarian dust
  spreading to the two capitals—
old official of the imperial retinue,
  ten thousand miles away,
came here when skies were cold,
  heard the sound of the river.

A Little Shower, Very Cool: in the Boat I Slept Soundly until Evening

(1178, sailing down the Yangtze. 7-ch. *chüeh-chü*; CNSK 10.)

In a boat one shower swept clear the swarming flies;
floppy hat half off, I stretch out on the green cane chair.
Back at last from pleasant dreams, sunlight in the window fad-
    ing,
now and then the sound of gentle sculling—downriver to
    Pa-ling.

In the Garden: Written at Random

(1179, fourth of four poems with this title. In the first two lines the poet seems to be recalling the happy days of his sojourn in Szechwan. A "poem bag" is a small bag used for storing drafts of poems. 7-ch. *chüeh-chü*; CNSK 11.)

Late blossoms left on the ground,
    shoots of bamboo poking up the mud;
the tea bowl, the poem bag—
    I took them wherever I went.
My dim dream just taking shape,
    who calls me back to waking?
By the window half in slanting sun
    a partridge cries.

A Chüeh-chü *to Record My Thoughts*

(1180, at Fu-chou in Kiangsi. T'ien-t'ai is a mountain range in Chekiang famous for its Buddhist and Taoist monasteries. First in a series of five, 7-ch.; CNSK 12.)

Thirty years since I've been to T'ien-t'ai;
the grass hut I still remember—we slept on the brink of
    clouds.
At dawn from the rows of pines an old priest appeared,
jug in hand, off to draw water from the rocky spring.

Little Garden

(1181, first and third of four poems with this title, written when the poet was in retirement at his old home in Shao-hsing. In the first, the poet is reading the works of T'ao Yüan-ming. 7-ch. *chü-eh-chü*; CNSK 13.)

I

Mist-veiled plants in the little garden
    reach to the house next door;
mulberry trees make deep shade,
    one small path slanting through.
I lie down to read T'ao's poems—
    less than one chapter,
when fine rain brings an excuse
    to jump up and hoe the melons.

II

In village south, village north,
    the wood-pigeons call;
water spikey with new seedlings,
    stretching calm into the distance.
Round the sky's edge I've traveled,
    a thousand, ten thousand miles,
now—of all things—I take lessons in spring planting
    from the old man next door.

Vegetable Garden

(1181; one mou is about one-seventh of an acre. 5-ch. *ku-shih*; CNSK 13.)

The old mountain man is learning to garden,
laughing at himself, wondering how he'll do.
Rocky barren ground, barely three mou—
for the heavy work I count on the two hired men.
Square plots laid out like a chessboard;
after a light shower, soil looks like melted butter.
We've hacked and cleared till all the brush and thorns are
        gone,
plowed and hoed till there's no more stones or clods,
laid a log bridge across the ditch,
built a little tower with broken tiles we gleaned,
on the unused land, set up poles for melons,
with the energy left over, planted a taro patch.
Like strands of silk—the thin greens growing;
like duck meat—the mushy steamed gourd.
Things such as these now I've learned to understand—
it was not for bream that I came back east.[1]

1. When the poet-official Chang Han (258?–319?) resigned his
post in the capital and retired, he said it was because he longed for
the bream he used to eat back home in the south.

In a boat on a summer evening,
I heard the cry of a water bird.
It was very sad and seemed to be saying,
"Madam is cruel!"
Moved, I wrote this poem.

(1183; Lu Yu was no doubt recalling his first wife whom he married when he was about twenty and divorced shortly afterwards, apparently because his mother found fault with the girl. He was very fond of her and wrote of her often in his poems.[1] 5-ch. *ku-shih;* CNSK 14.)

A girl grows up hidden in far-off rooms,
no glimpse of what may lie beyond her wall and hedge.
Then she climbs the carriage, moves to her new lord's home;
father and mother become strangers to her then.
    "I was stupid, to be sure, yet I knew
that Madam, my mother-in-law, must be obeyed.
Out of bed with the first cock's crowing,
I combed and bound my hair, put on blouse and skirt.
I did my work, tidied the hall, sprinkling and sweeping,
in the kitchen prepared their plates of food.
Green green the mallows and goosefoot I gathered—

1.   The most famous is probably that written in 1155 when Lu Yu chanced to meet his former wife, by then remarried, in the Shen family garden in Shao-hsing. The poem is in *tz'u* form (written to the tune "Hairpin Head Phoenix"), which uses lines of varying lengths and a broken, impressionistic style. In accordance with *tz'u* convention, it is written from the woman's point of view and de-

too bad I couldn't make them taste like bear's paws.[2]
When the least displeasure showed in Madam's face,
the sleeves of my robe were soon damp with tear stains.
My wish was that I might bear a son,
to see Madam dandle a grandson in her arms.
But those hopes in the end failed and came to nothing;
ill-fated, they made me the butt of slander.
Driven from the house, I didn't dare grumble,
only grieved that I'd betrayed Madam's kindness."
On the old road that runs along the rim of the swamp,
when fox fire glimmers through drizzling rain,
can you hear the voice crying "Madam is cruel!"?
Surely it's the soul of the wife sent home.

———————

scribes her sorrow, though it clearly reflects the anguished feelings
of the poet himself:

Pink tender hand,
     yellow *t'eng* wine,
city crammed with spring hues, willow by garden wall:
east winds hateful,
     the one I loved, cold—
a heart all sadness,
parted how many years?
     wrong! wrong! wrong!

Spring as always,
     someone grown needlessly thin,
tear stains wet the pink kerchief, soaking through mermaid's
     gauze.
Peach petals falling,
     stillness of a pond pavilion:
mountain-firm vows go on forever,
but a letter would be useless now—
     don't! don't! don't!

2. Bear's paws are the epitome of delicious food.

A Little Drink under the Moon

(1183, in Shao-hsing. 5-ch. *ku-shih*; CNSK 15.)

Last night, rain all around the eaves,
lone lamp before me, I sat scratching my head;
tonight moonlight floods the courtyard;
leaning on the old willow, I sing a long song.
The world's changes—huge and never-ending;
success/failure—one turn of the palm.
In man's life the happiest thing
is to lie and hear them pressing out the new wine.
Since I came home from Liang and Yi,
I grieve for kin and friends faded and fallen,
name after name marked down in the list of dead—
who can manage to hold out for long?
Most of the young fellows I don't even know—
what use would they have for a wreck like me?
One cup—no one to share it with—
I'll knock on the gate and call the old fellow next door.

For a week after Grain in Ear, it rained every day; suddenly I found myself with a long-lined poem.

(1185; Grain in Ear is one of the twenty-four divisions of the solar year, falling around June 6th; in south China it marks the beginning of the rainy season. Long-lined means a poem employing a seven-character line. 7-ch. *lü-shih;* CNSK 17.)

Grain in Ear just past, the rain arrives on time;
I rise from a nap in gauze curtains, pointed cap askew.
Stupid clouds refuse to scatter, forever pressing on the pagoda;
water in fields, soundless, finds its own way to the pond.
Green trees cool in evening, noisy with pigeon talk;
painted eaves quiet by day, the swallows late coming home.
Peaceful, I relish this total lack of anything to do,
robe draped on the perfume rack, singing poems to myself.[1]

1. When not being worn, robes were hung on a rack over an incense burner in order to scent them.

In the Boat, Three Chüeh-chü Expressing My Feelings, To Be Presented to His Excellency the Grand Tutor, with a Copy by Letter to the Palace Gentleman Yüeh Ta-yung.

(1185, the second of three poems. The "cold river" of the last line is probably the Ch'ien-t'ang, near Shao-hsing, which is subject to the ocean's tides. 7-ch. *chüeh-chü*; CNSK 17.)

Rain pelts the lone boat's awning, wine slowly wears off;
the fading lamp and I—both of us feeling low.
Fortune and fame never were things to be counted on,
not like the cold river's two tides each day.

Lin-an: Spring Rain Has Let Up at Last

(1186, when the poet journeyed to the capital, Lin-an (Hangchow), for an audience with the emperor on the occasion of his appointment to a post in Yen-chou in Chekiang. Clear Bright, one of the twenty-four divisions of the solar year, falls around April 5th. 7-ch. *lü-shih*; CNSK 17.)

Recent years my taste for the world grows thin as flimsy gauze;
who put me astride this horse, a visitor to the shining capital?
In a little tower all night I hear the spring rain;
tomorrow morning deep in the lanes they'll be peddling apricot flowers.
On short paper, lines askew, I scribble characters in grassy script;
by the fair weather window, tiny bubbles—I amuse myself making tea.
White robes—no need to worry they'll be blackened by wind and dust—
before Clear Bright Festival comes, I'll be back home again!

Autumn Thoughts

(1186, when Lu Yu was acting governor of Yen-chou. Second of two poems, 5-ch. *ku-shih;* CNSK 18.)

Mornings, up before the rooster calls;
evenings, never home till crows have gone to rest;
orders and commissions heaped on my desk,
napping and eating in the midst of them.
Flailing a whip, I press for tax payments,
squiggling my writing brush, face red with shame—
the bright day passes in a frenzy of action,
but what solace does this bring to the helpless and poor?
Leaves have fallen, the angling woods are bare;
trim and pretty as a hairdo—hills south of the valley.
It's not that I don't have my cup of wine for comfort,
but when will this press of business ever slacken?

The Merchant's Joy

(1187; 7-ch. *ku-shih* in *yüeh-fu* or ballad style; CNSK 19.)

The wide wide Yangtze, dragons in deep pools;
wave blossoms, purest white, leap to the sky.
The great ship, tall-towered, far off no bigger than a bean;
my wondering eyes have not come to rest when it's here be-
      fore me.
Matted sails: clouds that hang beyond the embankment;
lines and hawsers: their thunder echoes from high town
      walls.
Rumble rumble of ox carts to haul the priceless cargo;
heaps, hordes to dazzle the market—men race with the
      news.
In singing-girl towers to play at dice, a million on one throw;
by flag-flown pavilions calling for wine, ten thousand a cask;
the Mayor? the Governor? we don't even know their names;
what's it to us who wields power in the palace?
Confucian scholar, hard up, dreaming of one square meal;
a limp, a stumble, prayers for pity at His Excellency's gate;
teeth rot, hair falls out—no one looks your way;
belly crammed with classical texts, body lean with care—
See what Heaven gives me—luck thin as paper!
Now I know that merchants are the happiest of men.

It has snowed repeatedly and
      we can count on a good crop of wheat
      and barley; in joy I made this song.

(1187, at his post in Yen-chou. 7-ch. *ku-shih*; CNSK 19.)

Bitter cold, but don't complain when Heaven sends down
    snow;
snow comes to bring us next year's grain!
Third month: emerald waves dancing in the east wind;
fourth month: clouds of yellow hiding paths in the southern
    field.
How easy to see it—rows of houses raising shouts of joy,
already certain that officials will ease their load of taxes.
Sickle at waist, every young man in the village turns out;
gleaning kernels, little boys each day by the hundred and
    thousand.
Dust of white jade spills from the mill wheel, whirling up to
    the rafters;
noodles, silver threads into the pot, to be melted in boiling
    water.
Winter wine beginning to work, cakes of steamed malt burst-
    ing;
in oil pressed from fresh sesame, Cold Food dumplings smell-
    ing sweet; [1]

1. The dumplings were prepared ahead of time for the Cold
Food Festival, 105 days after the winter solstice, when all cooking
fires were put out.

the wife steps down from her loom, neglecting her morning
      weaving;
little sister helps in the kitchen, forgetful of evening makeup.
Old men, stuffed with food, laugh and thump their bellies;
under the trees, beating time on the ground, they sing of this
      season of peace.

Going to the Office

(1189, in the capital, where he held a post in the Board of Rites. 7-ch. *lü-shih;* CNSK 21.)

Dot on dot of frail petals drop into my cup of green wine;
lightly, lightly the lean horse tramps on through yellow dust.
Before my eyes, great lines of poetry, but I pass by as though
      they were nothing;
in dreams old friends now and then come to pay a call.
I ask to be sent to the border, the old madness still on me;
look at my graying beard in the mirror and feel the press of
      age.
This morning, pleasantly cool, papers to be dealt with are few;
I lean on my desk by the southern window, listen to the thun-
      der roll.

The Sound of Rain

(1191, back home in Shao-hsing. 7-ch. *ku-shih*; CNSK 24.)

Sound of rain, its tiny ticking, from dawn till evening:
in it hear the poet's song, far from dusty worlds.
"Cloud Gate," "Hsien Pond," muffled by a thousand years—
broken scores, forgotten notes—the clue to them lies here.[1]
Sound of rain, its tiny ticking, at night never ceasing:
in it hear the banished minister grieve as he quits his country,
long ridges of Nine Doubt Mountain, autumn by waters of the
    Hsiang,
fierce loyalty burning within, his tears tumbling down.[2]
Now I'm old and ailing, every thought gone from my head;
I lie facing the green lamp that coughs out its dying flame.
I lean on the bed and inhale, imitating a cold weather turtle;
propped on a pillow, humming long songs, I laugh to my
    lonely sword.
Sound of rain never lets up—sleep pleasanter than ever;

1. "Cloud Gate" and Hsien Pond" were musical compositions supposed to have been written by the Yellow Emperor in high antiquity but lost long ago. The poet suggests that something of their rare beauty is to be found in the sound of the rain.

2. The "banished minister" is the poet-statesman Ch'ü Yüan (3d cen. B.C.), who was exiled to the region of Chiu-i or Nine Doubt Mountain and the Hsiang River and eventually committed suicide there.

as the window whitens and crows caw, I get up and put on
    my robe,
call to my son to roast a rabbit, pour me some muddy wine,
then settle down in the folding chair amid the sound of rain.

Written in a Carefree Mood

(1192, in Shao-hsing, first of two poems with this title. The mummers of line four are villagers dressed up in costume who go from house to house at the beginning of spring driving out evil spirits. 5-ch. *lü-shih;* CNSK 26.)

Old man pushing seventy,
in truth he acts like a little boy,
whooping with delight when he spies some mountain fruits,
laughing with joy, tagging after village mummers;
with the others having fun stacking tiles to make a pagoda,
standing alone staring at his image in the jardiniere pool.
Tucked under his arm, a battered book to read,
just like the time he first set off for school.

Monk Halls

(1193; an attack on the sumptuousness of Buddhist temples. 7-ch. *ku-shih;* CNSK 27.)

Monk halls—wood and plaster daubed in gold and green;
in four directions go pleas for funds, urgent as a call to arms.
Rich merchants, great officials, wealth piled in heaps—
they can afford to throw away gold like so much gravel or
    tile.
But the poor man, his wife and child, rice eked out with
    beans—
one famine and they topple over, shrunken corpses in a ditch;
whipped and beaten at tax time, they bloody the magistrate's
    yard,
yet without regret they'll hand over what little they have to
    the monks!
The ancients watched over the people as one watches over a
    child,
encouraged them in farm tasks, worried they might suffer
    want;
open terrace at a hundred in gold—he wouldn't let it be
    built;
even his virtue ashamed beside the Duke of Chou's "Seventh
    Month" poem.[1]

1. Emperor Wen (r. 180–57 B.C.) of the Han planned to build a large open terrace but, told it would cost a hundred measures of gold, he abandoned the project as too extravagant. The Duke of Chou's poem is #154 in the *Book of Odes* and describes the agri-

Common fools, muddled and bemused—how could they un-
   derstand?
They see men maimed and mangled by the law, think it only
   right.
Till there's an end to huge halls, giant Buddha statues,
how can the weary people ever escape hunger and death?

cultural activities appropriate to the different months of the year.
It was supposedly written by the sage as a model of ideal agricul-
tural practices for his ward, the youthful King Ch'eng.

The Stone on the Hilltop

(1193; 5-ch. and 7-ch. *ku-shih;* CNSK 28.)

Autumn wind: ten thousand trees wither;
spring rain: a hundred grasses grow.
Is this really some plan of the Creator,
this flowering and fading, each season that comes?
Only the stone there on the hilltop,
its months and years too many to count,
knows nothing of the four-season round,
wearing its constant colors unchanged.
The old man has lived all his life in these hills;
though his legs fail him, he still clambers up,
now and then strokes the rock and sighs three sighs:
how can I make myself stony like you?

Separation

(1193; a wife longs for her husband who is off in Chiu-ch'üan in the northwest on a military campaign. 7-ch. *ku-shih* in *yüeh-fu* or ballad style; CNSK 28.)

Deep in lanes of the lonely city, autumn hushed and still,
the beautiful lady put down her shuttle, sighed in the night.
In the empty garden, dew wet the twigs of thorn and bramble;
on the overgrown path, moonlight lit the tracks of wildcat and
     fox.
"To think when you left the child was still in my belly—
now he skips like a calf, and his father doesn't even know!
The Purple Maiden's auspicious words never could be be-
     lieved;
how can I trust the tile oracle to tell me the day of return? [1]
Since I came as a bride I've never once gone beyond the gate;
how will my dreaming spirit find the way to Chiu-ch'üan?
No pumice and floss polish my mirror—I can't bear to see it
     shine.
A woman's good years number less than ten."

1. The Purple Maiden was a popular deity worshiped on the fif-
teenth night of the first month, when she was supposed to reveal
fortunes for the coming year. Another form of divination was
conducted by shamans who broke tiles and predicted the future
on the basis of the way they shattered.

Harp Song—To Send to Chi-ch'ang Shao-ch'ing

(1194; Chi-ch'ang is the poet's close friend Chang Yin. First of two poems; 5-ch. *ku-shih* in *yüeh-fu* or ballad style; CNSK 30.)

Not that the tree in my garden does not bloom,
but with frost-fall, its ten thousand leaves wither;
not that you would put me aside, my friend,
but as distance parts us, we grow naturally estranged.
In the night I get up, sighing,
open the box, dig for your old letters.
They're dark with dust and the bugs have chewed them,
lines missing, words about to fade.
I read them once and my face flushes,
read them again and tears begin to flow.
Roll them up, put them back in the box—
better to leave them for the silverfish to eat!

Mirror Lake

(1195; Mirror Lake was a sizable body of water by Lu Yu's home in Shao-hsing. In Sung times the edges of the lake were filled in and converted into paddy but, as the poem makes clear, the dikes that should have protected the fields had fallen into disrepair and the lake often overflowed. 5-ch. *ku-shih*; CNSK 32.)

I do my own farming, hope for a bellyful,
with worry and misgiving wait the good year,
but drought and flood come one on the heels of the other—
a bushel of rice costs close to a thousand cash!
Mirror Lake broke through its banks long ago,
but it wasn't Heaven first brought this trouble on.
Who'll try to trace the cause of it?
The old shape of the lake is still there to see.
Build up the low places, raise them higher,
heap on tiles to make the dikes firm—
then benefits of a thousand years can easily be rewon,
the builder's name handed down for all time.
But peasants in their ignorance can't understand,
and officials think only of getting through the days ahead;
and these words of mine will of course go unheeded—
the anger and fret of it won't let me sleep at night!

Beginning of Summer

(1195, ninth in a set of ten poems. The embankment is that of Mirror Lake; the Willow Maiden is a local deity, though nothing is known of her cult. Fang-weng is the literary name which Lu Yu adopted in 1176, meaning "the old man who does as he pleases." 7-ch. *chüeh-chü*; CNSK 32.)

On the overgrown embankment that stretches on and on,
>   east of the old floodgate,
the little shrine of the Willow Maiden
>   in the midst of willow shade.
Fang-weng, old and worn out,
>   leaning on a goosefoot cane,
still manages to trail along with the villagers,
>   going to pray for good crops.

Feeling Sorry for Myself

(1197; in the fifth month of this year, the poet's wife died at the age of seventy-one. 7-ch. *ku-shih*; CNSK 36.)

Morning rain, evening rain, little plums turned yellow;
in house to the east, house to the west, orchids for sale smell-
      ing sweet;
old white-headed widower mourning in an empty hall,
wailing not for the dead alone—feeling sorry for himself as
      well,
teeth like battered clogs, hair resembling frost—
going by his looks, how can he last much longer?
Lean on my stick, try to get up, but I fall back on the bed
      each time;
death draws near me, hardly a wall away.
Ten thousand affairs of the world all dim and far removed,
my only thought to advance in virtue—that's what I work
      at now.
If I follow the two brothers to starve on Shou-yang Mountain,
a thousand years, bones rotted, I'll still have the fragrance of a
      good name.[1]

1. Po Yi and Shu Ch'i, brothers in ancient times who chose to starve to death on Shou-yang Mountain rather than compromise with the evil of the world, are familiar symbols of stern integrity and fidelity to one's ideals.

Sitting Outdoors

(1198; the poet was receiving a government pension in the form of grain. Second of two poems; 7-ch. *lü-shih;* CNSK 37.)

Cap tipped back, propped by a window, still can't settle
    down;
haul out the cane of Ch'iung bamboo, take a turn in the gar-
    den.
Clear autumn coming on—dew soaks the grass;
bright moon not yet risen—stars crowd the sky.
Barges shove through lock gates, racing for dawn markets;
men on treadmills watering fields—no night's sleep for
    them!
Plain people sweating like this for one square meal,
and I sit eating government dole—wince whenever I think
    of it.

Year of Plenty

(1198; 7-ch. *lü-shih;* CNSK 37.)

Year of plenty—its joyous sound rocks the four directions;
late autumn sunshine sparkles like a day in spring.
With lamb sausage, lugging wine, grooms race off to greet
      brides;
lizard-skin drums, dragon boats—all join in celebration of
      the gods.
Everywhere they're happy clear weather's come on *chia-tzu*
      day;
home after home aims for *keng-shen* to begin new building.[1]
Old man, hoping to join in community drinking bouts,
first gets dressed up in a long robe trimmed with a purple col-
      lar.

1. If in autumn the day *chia-tzu* of the sixty-day cycle is clear, it
portends a good rice crop; the day *keng-shen* of the cycle is con-
sidered propitious for beginning construction work on a house.

The rain cleared and the breeze and sunshine are superb as I stroll outside the gate.

(1201, third of three poems. A note by the poet explains that Chang and Wu were neighbors who both died in the winter of the previous year. 7-ch. *chüeh-chü*; CNSK 45.)

Old man Chang, sick three years, finally up and died;
Grandpa Wu in one evening went where he couldn't hear us
   calling.
I alone, with this body tough as iron,
leaning by the gate, always looking at the green of evening
   hills.

My Village Home

(1201, second of two poems; 5-ch. *lü-shih;* CNSK 47.)

Living's getting harder day by day—
my house just goes on staying half finished.
Flapping like butterflies—torn window paper;
cracked like a turtle shell—dried mud walls.
In a light rain the cow pen turns soggy;
a touch of frost and the mill shed feels cold.
But the late grain at least is spared from insects—
neighbors and I all sigh with relief.[1]

1. A note by the poet says: "This year the late grain was badly damaged by insects—only our village was spared."

Sending Tzu-lung
Off to a Post in Chi-chou

(1202; Tzu-lung was the poet's second son, who was on his way to the post of judge in Chi-chou in Kiangsi. 5-ch. *ku-shih*; CNSK 50.)

I'm old and you're going away—
you have no choice, I know.
From the carriage I see you off,
brushing away tears I can't hold back.
Who likes to say good-by?
But we're poor and have to do these things.
You will brave the billows of Hsü,[1]
from there cross Lake P'eng-li,
waves alive with boat-swallowing fish,
forests shrill with one-legged goblins.
Rice you eat in fields—what inn will cook it?
Scull of your lone boat—by what banks will it rest?
A judge—better than T'ang times;
at least you'll be spared the whip.[2]
Line up and bow with the others—no shame in that;
to slack your job—that's the only disgrace.
You'll be an official of Chi-chou;

1. High waves on the Ch'ien-t'ang River, where the body of the loyal minister Wu Tzu-hsü was cast in ancient times. According to legend, he became the god of the waves and his anger causes the tidal bore that rages up the river.

2. In T'ang times the head of the local government could whip his subordinate officials, but this was forbidden under the Sung.

see you drink no more than Chi-chou water!
When you know where every penny goes,
who can find excuse for talk?
Set aside a little for A-hsi's wedding,
find a good tutor for Yüan-li.[3]
I can keep myself in food;
don't worry about fancy things for me.
My robe wears through?—let the elbows stick out;
shoes come apart?—leave the toes showing;
out the gate I may be laughed at;
back home, I'll sleep better for it.
Lord Yi, a man of name and station,[4]
solid—stands out like a mountain peak;
his family and ours have been friends for generations—
perhaps he'll grant you an interview.
If so, count that honor enough—
in no way must you seem to be courting favor!
Again there's Yang Ch'eng-chai; [5]
no one these days his match for integrity;
the kind who hears one stupid word
and spends three days washing out his ears.
You may go and see how he's getting on,
but end it there—no further talk!
Hsi-chou I've known for years,
Ching-ssu comes from our home town; [6]

3. Tzu-lung's daughter and eldest son respectively.

4. Lord Yi is Chou Pi-ta, friend of the poet and former prime minister, who was living in retirement at Chi-chou.

5. The poet and statesman Yang Wan-li (1127–1206), also living in retirement.

6. Ch'en Hsi-chou and Tu Ssu-kung (Ching-ssu) were friends of the poet who were apparently serving as officials in Chi-chou.

not only do they excel in letters;
in action and character equally fine.
Study and learn all you can from them—
achievement lies in piling up!
"Benevolence," "righteousness"—take them where you find
     them;
in practice they make the gentleman.
Three years and you'll be home again;
who knows—I may still be here.
There are carp in the rivers where you're going—
give them a letter to carry now and then.[7]

7. An allusion to an old *yüeh-fu* ballad that tells of a gift of a pair of carp, in the belly of one of which was found a letter. In T'ang times, letters were folded into the shape of a pair of fish.

The hsiu-ts'ai *Tu Shu-kao* dropped in on me in a snow storm, spent the night, and then went on. I composed this poem to send him off.

(1202; Tu Shu-kao or Tu Yu was a young poet from Chin-hua in Chekiang. The title *hsiu-ts'ai* indicates that he has passed the provincial examination; the "ten thousand books" of the last line are presumably the works he studied in order to pass the exam. 7-ch. *lü-shih*; CNSK 50.)

Take a long trip—then you learn how hard the road can be,
through border mountains that have no end, waters trackless
    and wide.
Wind about to blow you over, the lonely city still a long way
    off;
snow hissing down as from a sieve, the country temple cold;
at evening, lugging a clothes sack, you put in at my dirt-
    walled lodge,
at dawn bought village wine, slung it from your donkey sad-
    dle.
Not one word of your writings do men really understand;
what a waste—the ten thousand books wrapped up in your
    breast!

Living in the Village,
Writing of My Joys

(1202, 7-ch. *lü-shih;* CNSK 50.)

Plum Town's red bridge, dawn mountains sprawling;
Fan River's white pagoda, spring waters on the rise;
breath of blossoms strikes us, we realize how warm it's gotten;
magpie voices thread the trees, happy at a new clear spell.
In the town square, wine's cheap—even poor people can get
    drunk;
in country fields, lots of mud—even an old man can plow it.
Pleasantest of all, to think taxes have been paid on time—
for this year at least, no officials banging at my wicker gate.

Spring Festival Days: Imitating the Style of the Master of Wan-ling

(1203; the spring festival was held at the village shrine on the day with the cyclical sign *mou* that fell nearest the vernal equinox. The Master of Wan-ling is the famous Northern Sung poet Mei Yao-ch'en (1002–1060), whose work Lu Yu admired. First and fourth of four poems; 5-ch. *ku-shih*; CNSK 53.)

I   Festival Rain

No time at all since the year began,
suddenly Spring Festival's upon us.
Stretching on forever, the grasses' deepening color;
hsiao-hsiao, the sound of rain growing shriller;
steering his plow, ambling the bright water,
what does he care if straw sandals get soggy?
Village boys have an even better time,
barefoot, standing tall on the water ox's back.

II   Festival Meat

Festival day, they pounce on the shrine pig,
roast it over coals—the good smell fills the village!
Hungry crows flock to roadside trees;
old shamans station themselves by the shrine gate.
Though it's nothing grand like a *hsing* or *lao*,
still there's something of the old ways here.[1]
Drunk and heading home, I pocket the leftovers,
a little treat to pass around among the grandchildren.

1.   *Hsing* and *lao* were sacrifices performed by the Son of Heaven and feudal lords in ancient times involving a variety of sacrificial animals.

Autumn Thoughts

(1203; Ping was a region famous for its swords. First of three, 7-ch. *chüeh-chü*; CNSK 54.)

Sumac showing pale traces of red,
    chrysanthemums bit by bit unfurling;
a tall sky where winds keep company
    with the sadness of wild goose cries—
my poems—have they not a keenness
    to match the blades of Ping?
They slice off a bit of autumn scene,
    wrap it up in a paper scroll.

Chüeh-chü

(Sixth in a set of twelve *chüeh-chü* written in the eighth month of the year *chia-tzu*, 1204. 7-ch; CNSK 58.)

My medicine's crude, yet the old farmer
    swears it really works;
my poems are shallow, yet the mountain monk
    has immoderate praise for their skill.
Cakes in pockets, with packets of tea
    they come to pay me a visit.
What harm if in the midst of loneliness
    we have one little laugh?

Moved by Memories of the Past

(1204; the poet is recalling the period around 1158–59 when he held a post at Ning-te in Fukien. The island he saw is probably Taiwan, which at this time was considered part of the Liuchiu or Ryukyu Islands. First of a set of five, 7-ch. *chüeh-chü*; CNSK 59.)

When I was about thirty I remember traveling south,
in a ten thousand bushel boat calmly sailing the wide sea.
Always I recall, when early autumn thunderstorms had
    cleared,
the helmsman explaining, pointing a finger: "The Ryukyus
    there!"

Since the beginning of the year
the overcast weather and rain have
continued for days without letting up.

(1205; Shan-yin is the area in Shao-hsing where Lu Yu lived. 7-ch. *lü-shih;* CNSK 61.)

River clouds endlessly rolling, rain dense and dark;
old, I came home to Shan-yin to learn how to water a garden.
Ten li, twisty as sheepgut—the road barely goes through;
three houses, legs of a kettle—that's what our "village" is
    made of.
In proper season, New Year's noodles—I go along with cus-
    tom;
Chung K'uei who's borne up so long—you must go on
    glowering at my gate.[1]
Report comes from nearby districts, lots of robbers these
    days—
I tell the boys to pack in thorns, patch the holes in the fence.

1. Pictures of the demon-queller Chung K'uei were pasted on the gate for protection. It was the custom to remove the old pictures and replace them with new ones at the New Year, but a note by the poet explains that this year he was too poor to make the change.

Poorer than usual, I made these Chüeh-chü *as a joke.*

(1205; eighth in a set of eight. Though the poet's family were farmers, they were sometimes obliged to buy rice in order to get by. 7-ch. *chüeh-chü;* CNSK 63.)

Someone went to buy rice, late getting back,
    noon and it still isn't cooked;
though they don't let on, my family worries
    that the old man must be starving.
They don't know I'm by the eastern window
    fiddling with a brush,
just in the middle of writing a poem to match
    Yüan-ming's "Begging for Food." [1]

1. A poem by T'ao Yüan-ming describing his extreme poverty. Lu Yu was passing the time by writing a poem using the same rhymes as T'ao's original.

I had occasion to tell a visitor about an old trip I took through the gorges of the Yangtze.

(1205; the poet is recalling the time in 1170 when he traveled up the Yangtze to a post in K'uei-chou; Chien-p'ing is a little east of K'uei-chou. There were many non-Chinese peoples living in the region. 7-ch. *ku-shih*; CNSK 63.)

Long ago I made that journey, fall rain coming down lightly,
reached the east wall of Chien-p'ing just as gates were closing.
Host at the inn met me with greetings, words rambling on and
    on,
his young wife grinding and cooking in her cheap white robe.
Old boatmen who work the river, some drunk, some sobered
    up;
merchants from Shu, peddlers of the gorges, clever at closing a
    deal;
soon lamps went dark, people getting ready for bed,
though outside we could still hear boats tying up, baggage
    being unloaded from horses.
Mountains steep, rivers treacherous, barbarian tribes close by;
often I saw their mallet-shaped hairdos mingling with city
    folk.
Now, counting on my fingers, I find it's been forty years!—
sad memories held in my heart, truly from another incarnation.

Strange Dream

(1208; the poet, savoring six place names from the north, dreams of the time when the Chin invaders will be driven out and China united once more. 5-ch. *lü-shih;* CNSK 77.)

Here in the hills I had a strange dream:
in ponderous armor, I waved a carved lance,
where Fu waters flow west into the Wei,
and T'ung Pass to the north guards the Yellow River;
sadly the lutes of Chao sang,
bravely the songs of Yen joined in.
These things in the end will come about—
when I'm dead and gone, but that can't be helped.

Midautumn: on Something That Happened

(1208; sixth of a set of ten, 7-ch. *chüeh-chü*; CNSK 78.)

Habits of a man of letters—I've shed them all at last;
no wine fever, no poetry passion to seize me now.
Don't be surprised this morning, though, if I take up ink stone
     and brush;
villagers want me to write them a locust-expelling charm.

Farm Families

(1208; first and sixth in a set of six, 5-ch. *lü-shih*; CNSK 78.)

I

Snug—the robe sewn from coarse cotton;
red—the fire kindled from dry sticks.
Meager talents I give to the countryside;
simple learning I teach the young boys:
for sheep you want a pen that's high,
for chickens, a closely woven basket.
Farm families have joys of their own,
not in a class with those of kings.

II

It's late, the children come home from school;
braids unplaited, they ramble the fields,
jeering at each other—guess what's in my hand!
arguing—who won the grass fight after all?
Father sternly calls them to lessons;
grandfather indulgently feeds them candy.
We don't ask you to become rich and famous,
but when the time comes, work hard in the fields!

Sitting Up at Night

(1208; 7-ch. *chüeh-chü*; CNSK 79.)

Spinners' lights from house to house brighten the deep night;
here and there new fields have been plowed after rain.
Always I feel ashamed to be so old and idle.
Sitting close by the stove, I hear the sound of the wind.

To Show to My Sons

(1209; Lu Yu's deathbed poem. The Nine Provinces are the divisions of China in ancient times. 7-ch. *chüeh-chü*; CNSK 85.)

In death I know well enough all things end in emptiness;
still I grieve that I never saw the Nine Provinces made one.
On the day the king's armies march north to take the heart-
    land,
at the family sacrifice don't forget to let your father know.

Diary of a Trip to Shu
(Excerpts from the Ju-Shu-chi)

Ch'ien-tao 5th year (1169), 12th month, 6th day: I received word of appointment as vice-governor of K'uei-chou. Since I'm just now recovering from a long illness and can't undertake such a lengthy journey, I plan to put off my departure until the beginning of autumn.

Ch'ien-tao 6th year (1170), 6th month, 1st day: Early in the morning we shifted the boat and went through the lock [from Lin-an into the Grand Canal]. It took us nearly all of one day before we got through the third lock. Boats are as thick as teeth in a comb. It is terribly hot, and though it rained a little after noon, the heat did not let up. We tied up in front of the rice trading area.

3d day: By dawn we reached Long River Bank, where there is a little market with lots of fish and crabs. After noon we reached Ch'ung-te District of Hsiu-chou. The district magistrate Wu Tao-fu, his assistant Li Chih, and the tax supervisor of Hsiu-chou Chang Shih came to see me. I had once heard from Tai Tzu-wei about a merchant of Ch'ung-te named Wu Yin who one day suddenly left his home and went to live in an inn. All day he sat silently in one room, nothing in the room but a single bed. When visitors came, he'd have them sit on the bed beside him; if they came with wine, he wouldn't refuse their visits but would spend the whole day with them in lively conversation. Wu Yin had originally not been a man of learning, but when he moved to the inn, he began discussing questions of divination and fate with others, and his remarks were always very perceptive. He could predict men's fortunes and life span, though no one could ever discern how he did it, I was told. I now took advantage of this opportunity to ask Magistrate Wu about the story, and he replied that it was all true. He said that the man had since moved and was not living in a country village.

This evening we went eighteen li.[1] We spent the night at Stone Gate. The fiery clouds are piled up like mountains and I know it's going to be a hot day tomorrow.

4th day: Very hot. Only in the afternoon did we begin to get a little breeze. In the evening we tied up in front of the Temple of Original Enlightenment. The temple was formerly the Hall of the Sacred Empyrean, but was burned in wartime. After the *chien-yen* era (1127–1130), it was rebuilt, but even now it is still very crude. By the temple's west verandah there is a lotus pond over ten mou in area,[2] with a flying bridge and a little pavilion, all very neat and lovely. In the pond are countless turtles—when they hear people talking they all come flocking around, sticking up their necks and peering at you. The boys [3] tried to frighten them, but they wouldn't be driven off.

7th day: We said good-by to all our friends and went to Fang Wu-te's place for a simple vegetarian meal. In the evening we shifted the boat out of the city [of Hsiu-chou] and tied up at the Flourishing Grain Hall, a very large and imposing building. It's been raining hard all day without letting up.

1. One li is about one third of a mile.

2. One mou is about one seventh of an acre.

3. Lu Yu's sons, of which he had four, or possibly five, at this time, the eldest twenty-two.

I sent for a doctor named Ch'iang to examine my family and T'ao.[4]

8th day: The rain has cleared and it is very cool—like late autumn. We now have the wind with us and the boatmen for the first time have hoisted the sail. We passed Joined Roads. There are many people living around here, most of them engaged in selling salted fish. Along the road many army horses are grazing. The water of the canal has overflowed and is standing several feet deep in the fields of the villages nearby. On both banks all the water wheels are being used to pump out the accumulation of water. The women and boys are working as hard as they can, and in some places oxen are used to turn the wheels. The women work the water wheels with their feet, while with their hands they go on spinning hemp. When we passed Level View we ran into heavy rain and violent wind and the whole inside of the boat got doused. After a little while, it cleared up. We spent the night at Eight Feet, where I heard that one of the boats traveling in the area had capsized and sunk. There are little boats that go around pounding on the gunwales and selling fish at a very cheap price. The mosquitoes are as fierce as hornets or scorpions!

9th day: Clear and windy. The boatmen, wary of repeating yesterday evening's near disaster, were unwilling to cast off the lines. Only after the sun was high in the sky did we get underway. We have come from Ch'ung-te across the big lake, and now for the first time we are able to see the distant mountains around Lake Chen. About noon we reached Wu River District and crossed the Pine River. The wind is very calm.

4. A servant? I have failed to discover the identity of T'ao or T'ung, mentioned on p. 72.

Through the introduction of Marshal Chou, I was able to summon a doctor named Cheng Tuan-ch'eng to examine the pulse of T'ung and T'ao. It seems they are both suffering from the heat. The salted fish we bought in the market turned out to be very tasty. In the evening we untied the boat and went out to the middle of the water to look around at the long bridge and many-storied pagoda. The misty waves stretch far into the distance and the whole scene looks like a painting. We spent the night at Yin Bridge and I climbed up on the bridge to look at the moon.

10th day: We reached P'ing-chiang (Soochow), but because we had sick people aboard, we did not enter the city. Instead we followed the wall around past P'an Gate, where we could see the pagoda of Wu-ch'iu-lou in the distance. It looks exactly like the Precious Forest Temple at home and gave me a twinge of nostalgia. We spent the night in front of the Maple Bridge Temple, of which the T'ang poet wrote:

"The sound of its midnight bells comes to the traveler's boat." [5]

11th day: At fifth watch (4 A.M.) we left Maple Bridge and by dawn had passed Riverbank Villa. There are a great many people living in this area. When we reached Vista Pavilion we stopped for a short rest. From here on, the water is flanked by long hills and tall embankments. There are many dry fields planted in beans and millet, and here and there dense bushes and thickets of bamboo, so that you feel as though you are being squeezed and suffocated—not at all like the area east of Maple Bridge. Only when we got to the vicinity of Wu-hsi or No Tin District did it become a little more level and open.

5. The poet Chang Chi (8th cen.) in a famous 7-ch. *chüeh-chü* entitled "Tying Up at Night at Maple Bridge."

We tied up at night at the district lodge.[6] Near the city is Tin Mountain, from which tin can be mined. Toward the end of the Han dynasty (2d cen. A.D.), there was a written prophecy which declared: "While there's tin, war in the world; no tin, the world at rest! While there's tin, struggle in the world; no tin, the world at peace!" From that time until now, whenever any tin comes to light people immediately bury it and are afraid to use it.

13th day: Early in the morning we entered Ch'ang-chou and tied up at the Ching Valley Lodge. At night the moon was as bright as day and I went for a walk with my family in the moonlight outside the post horse lodge. T'ao is beginning to improve.

16th day: We got an early start from Tan-yang. I dipped up some water from the Jade Milk Well. The well is at the Kuan-yin Temple beside the road and is listed in the "Classification of Waters." [7] The water is milky in color, sweet, and so cold it sets your teeth on edge. There is a plaque over the well written by Lord Ch'en Wen-chung,[8] the characters in molded jade in the "eight part" style of calligraphy. In front of the temple is the Lien Light Pavilion, which looks down on Lake Lien. It is a beautiful spot and hardly any distance at all

6. The *yi* or post horse lodge attached to the government office, at which officials could stay when traveling on business.

7. A list of wells, springs, and streams whose waters are most suitable for making tea. Two such lists, probably those which Lu Yu was familiar with, are found in a brief work entitled *Chien-ch'a shui-chi* (Record of waters for boiling tea) by Chang Yu-hsin (9th cen.), preserved in *Shuo-fu* ch. 81.

8. Ch'en Yao-sou, an official who received the *chin-shih* degree in the period 988–89.

from the government highway, and yet very few people ever come here to visit. Today I noticed that the blossoms of the silk tree are just now opening. At home, they have already been open for over a month—that's how much difference there is in the climate!

We passed Twin Hills, where there are two stone figures of human beings, one standing on each hill. People call them the Stone Old Man and the Stone Old Woman—actually they are statues marking the entrance to some ancient gravemound.

This stretch of the canal from the Ch'ien-t'ang River to Chen-chiang was not suitable for water transport in Liang and Ch'en times and before. It was Emperor Yang of the Sui (r. 605–617) who first dug a canal to cover these eight hundred li. The canal is uniformly ten chang in width,[9] with ridges running along both sides like a range of hills. These were formed by the accumulation of earth that was dug out. The fact that our dynasty was able to establish a temporary residence for the sovereign at Ch'ien-t'ang (Lin-an) was due solely to the existence of this canal. The Pien Canal [10] and this one were both created at the hands of the Sui dynasty, and both have turned out to be of great use to our own Sung—as though Fate had planned it that way!

We passed Hsin-feng and stopped for a little rest. Even today the city has a large population and numerous shops and

9. One chang is ten ch'ih or Chinese feet in length; the ch'ih is about three fourths of an English foot.

10. The canal leading south from the Northern Sung capital at Pien-ching (K'ai-feng) to the Yangtze. The Sung emperor and his court fled south on the canal from the Chin invaders, eventually establishing a capital euphemistically called a "temporary residence" at Lin-an or Hangchow.

markets. By night we arrived outside the city of Chen-chiang.[11] Today was the beginning of autumn.

19th day: Pao-yin, the head priest of Gold Mountain Temple, came to visit me. His polite name is T'an-shu and he is a native of Chia-chou. He says that from Hsia-chou on west, there are so many rapids in the Yangtze that it's impossible to count them all.

I went to dinner with Magistrate Ts'ai at the Tan-yang Tower. It was unspeakably hot, and though heaps of ice were placed beside each seat, they didn't make us feel the least bit cool. Ts'ai himself prepared tea for us, a task at which he is very skillful, though the tea was surprisingly bad. One of the other guests, a Professor Hsiung who is a native of Chien-ning (in Fukien) tells me that it has always been the custom to mix Fukien tea with rice powder. Recently, people have taken to adding wild yams and in the last two years they have further added the buds of paper mulberry, so that all these ingredients have gotten mixed up with the taste of the tea, which moreover has a lot of froth in it. Only after the rainy season has passed does it lose the flavor of these added ingredients. If one were not thoroughly acquainted with tea he could not easily detect all this.

In the late afternoon we moved the boat, went out through the third lock, and stopped when we reached Tide Lock.

23d day: I went to the Sweet Dew Temple and made an offering of a meal for the monks. Sweet Dew is on Pei-ku Mountain, and there is a stone called Wolf Stone. Popular tradition says that Emperor Chao-lieh of the (Minor) Han and the

11. Where the Grand Canal meets the Yangtze. From here on, the poet is traveling west on the Yangtze.

Great Emperor of Wu once sat on this stone and together planned an attack on Ts'ao Ts'ao.[12] The original stone disappeared long ago, but the monks immediately got another stone to put in its place, a process they have repeated several times. When visitors pat the stone and give great meaningful sighs, the monks and novices are often to be seen laughing behind their hands.

I paid my respects at the shrine of Li Wen-jang [13] and climbed the Many View Tower. The tower likewise is not the original building or site, but was built by the chief monk Hua-chao. As you look down on the great river, you can actually count the trees and grasses of Huai-nan on the farther shore. In fact this tower provides a finer view than the old one did.

27th day: I am staying at Gold Mountain Temple and it is very cool and pleasant. The head priest Pao-yin tells me that the egrets of Liang-shan-chün in Shu are the most beautiful in the world.

28th day: I got up early so I could watch the sun rise over the river. The sky and water were completely red—truly a splendid sight! While I was about it, I climbed Hero Stride Tower to look at the two islands. The one on the left is called Peregrine Hill because in old times there were said to be peregrines nesting there, though none live there now. The one on the right is called Cloud Root Island. Both stick up out of the water and are not attached to the land.

12. In the so-called Three Kingdoms period (220–265), when the empire was divided into the states of Shu (Minor Han) in the west, Wu in the south, and Wei in the North. Ts'ao Ts'ao (155–220) was the founder of the Wei.

13. The T'ang statesman Li Te-yü (787–849).

Around noon we passed Kua-chou. The river is as smooth as a mirror. From the boat I looked back at Gold Mountain with its jumble of towers and halls—indeed a sight of superb beauty. In the middle of the river we ran into severe wind and thunder, and a flash of lightning came leaping over the surface of the water not more than a chang or so from the boat. We tied up on the shore as fast as we could, and then suddenly it cleared and we went on to Kua-chou. Since we reached Chen-chiang there haven't been any mosquitoes, but this evening there are a great many of them and I will have to start putting up the net again.

29th day: Tied up at Kua-chou. The air is very clear and fresh. Looking south to Chen-chiang, I can see the Moon Tower, the Sweet Dew Temple, and the Water Office Shrine, all as though they were close by. Closest of all is Gold Mountain—I can even make out the peoples' eyes and eyebrows. And yet you can't cross the river here—you have to take the boat some distance upriver to the west before you can get across. Hence people who are crossing over always have to go considerably out of their way.

Because the sail was damaged, the boatmen went to Ku-su to buy a new sail and just got back today.[14] During these past two days I have been observing the people going back and forth across the river—there have been about a thousand persons, most of them soldiers. At night I can see the lights in the pagoda at Gold Mountain.

7th month, 1st day: At daybreak we left Kua-chou. The wind was with us and we put up the sail. By evening we

14. A note in the text, probably by the writer himself, states: "The mast is 5 chang 6 ch'ih tall (42 feet); the sail is 26 fu." A fu is a little over two ch'ih.

reached Chen-chou and tied up at the Pavilion for Scanning the Distance.

4th day: The wind is with us and we cast off the lines, hoisted the sail, and set out from Chen-chou. Along the bank there are great crowds of boats setting out one after another. Their misty sails stand out against the mountains, stretching far into the distance like a painting. After a while, the wind blew harder and the boat moved along very fast. We passed Melon Port Mountain. The mountain wiggles and winds its way up and down, following the edge of the river and rising in small peaks that stick straight up.

At evening we tied up at Little Bamboo Harbor. There are something over twenty families living here. We are thirty li from Chin-ling (Nanking).

11th day: We got an early start from the inlet and moved out into the big river, passing Three Mountain Point, Rapid Shoals, Kind Mother Point, and Colored Rock Bastion, tying up at the river mouth at T'ai-p'ing-chou. All the places where the mountains come right to the edge of the river are called "points." The water flows past them very swiftly and it is all the oarsmen can do, pitching in their strength and pulling, to get us past them. Because of the intercalated month this year, it is now early autumn and the water has already fallen several feet, so one can imagine what it must be like at the height of summer.

Today the wind was with us and we hoisted the sail and sounded our drums as we moved along. There were two big boats coming downriver to the east which, because the wind was against them, had to tie up in a cove. When the occupants saw us, they were furious and stamped their feet and shouted endless curses at us. Our boatmen made no reply, but only clapped their hands and roared with laughter, banging on the drums harder than ever and looking very pleased with themselves. This is always the way when people are held up or make good time on the river—those who have the wind with them act very proud of themselves and those who have it against them get angry. Both, of course, are at fault. There are so many occasions in life when we behave in the same way that I have recorded the incident here in hopes of providing a little laugh.

Colored Rock is also called Ox Beach and is directly across the river from Ho-chou. The river is narrower at this point than at Kua-chou and therefore when the Sui general Han Ch'in-hu marched south to attack the Ch'en, and when Ts'ao Pin of our own dynasty marched south to put down the Southern T'ang, they both crossed over at this point.[15] But even a gentle wind will immediately stir up the waves and make the river impassable.

It was at this point that Fan Jo-ping of the Southern T'ang planned the building of a pontoon bridge for the Sung ruler's armies to cross over. Earlier Jo-ping, having failed to win favor with the Southern T'ang ruler Li Yü (937–978), had cut his hair and pretended to become a monk, building a hut at Colored Rock Mountain. There he chiseled a hole through the rock and built a little stone pagoda, and at night when the moon was bright he would tie a rope to the hole in the pagoda

15. Han Ch'in-hu, acting in the name of Emperor Wen, the founder of the Sui, led the attack against the Ch'en, which had its capital at Nanking, in 589, thus uniting north and south China after almost three hundred years of separation. Ts'ao Pin (931–999) performed a similar service for the founder of the Sung by marching south in 974 to overthrow the state known as the Southern T'ang, which likewise had its capital at Nanking.

and row as fast as he could across the river in a little boat, pulling the rope across to the northern shore and in this way measuring the width of the river. When he had done this enough times to make certain there was no error in his measurements, he fled north to the Sung capital and submitted a letter to the throne with his proposal for a bridge. Later, the ruler's armies marched south and crossed the river, and the pontoon bridge they constructed was found to be exactly the right length down to the very inch.[16]

I might note here that Emperor Yang of the Sui, when he attacked Korea, used the same method in crossing the Liao River.[17] He had three pontoon bridges constructed on the west bank of the river, and when they were completed, had them dragged across to the east bank. But his bridges turned out to be a chang or so too short. The Sui soldiers had to jump into the water and fight their way against the Korean soldiers lined up on the bank waiting to attack them. After the Sui general Mai T'ieh-chang was killed in the fighting, the soldiers were finally called in and the bridges pulled back to the west bank. Ho Ch'ou was then commanded to make the bridges longer, a task which he completed in two days, and the army was at last able to cross the river. The Sui, however, was never able to conquer Korea, whereas our own dynasty succeeded in overthrowing the Southern T'ang. In fact, everything depends on the will of Heaven—Fan Jo-ping could not have changed things one way or the other.

16. The Sung army crossed the river late in 974 and captured Chin-ling, the capital of the Southern T'ang.

17. In 612 Emperor Yang in person led an expedition against the Korean state of Koguryŏ which ended in total failure, as did a second expedition the following year.

When Fan Jo-ping escaped to the north, everyone south of the Yangtze knew that he had presented a plan for an expedition against the region and there were those who requested that his mother and wife be executed in retaliation. Li Yü, however, did not venture to do so, but merely had them placed in confinement at Ch'ih-chou. Later, Jo-ping revealed the fact that his mother and wife were still in the south, and the Sung court ordered Li Yü to have them sent north under escort. He was furious, but in the end did not dare disobey the order; instead he treated the women generously and sent them on their way. The hole in the rock and the stone pagoda which Jo-ping had made, however, were left as they were, and when our armies marched south they used the hole to attach the rope of the pontoon bridge to—from this one can see what stupid and negligent rulers Li Yü and his ministers were! Even if there had been no Fan Jo-ping, how could he have survived? Chang Lei [18] wrote a "Discussion of the Conquest of the South" in which he says that Fan Jo-ping should have been shackled and sent back to Li Yü so that the latter could satisfy his desire for revenge; or, if this was not done, he should have been charged with the crime of betraying his lord and put to death as an example to the world. I find Chang Lei's opinion highly admirable—truly a model of correct thinking.

I have been sick ever since I got to Chin-ling, but today I seem to be a little better, though I still can't eat. It rained at night.

13th day: In the afternoon I entered the city of T'ai-p'ing-chou and visited the governor, Chou Yüan-t'e. He called a doctor named Kuo, who came immediately to the room where

18. 1054–1114, a scholar and official.

we were sitting, examined me, and discussed the merits of the medicine I am using.

The city is situated on the north bank of the Ku-shu River, which the local people call simply Ku River. The water of the river is pure green and as clear and lucid as a mirror—you can count the tiny fishes swimming up and down. The families on the south side of the river are all fishermen and the scenery is quite wonderful. There are two pontoon bridges outside the city, one going to Hsüan-ch'en, the other to Che-chung. Ku-shu Hall is said to be the best place to observe the beauty of the hills along the river, but right now there happens to be a traveler staying there so I wasn't able to visit it. There is also a wine tower which has an excellent view from its upper story. All these places are south of the city. In the old days a branch of the river used to run through the city, but it silted up long ago. In recent years there has been an attempt to dredge it out and get it running again, but it only flows for a little while in the spring and summer. Since it is now the seventh month, the flow has already dried up.

In Li Po's collected works there are "Ten Poems on Ku-shu." My father's elder second cousin Yen-yüan once told me the following anecdote. When Su Tung-p'o was on his way home from Huang-chou, he passed this way and, reading the poems, clapped his hands, gave a loud laugh, and said, "You can always spot a fake! How could Li Po have written anything like this?" Kuo Kung-fu [19] argued that the poems were genuine, whereupon Tung-p'o laughed again and said, "Then I'm afraid they must be by Li Po's later incarnation." Kung-fu was extremely put out at this. The reason was that, when he

19. Kuo Hsiang-cheng, a poet and official contemporary with Su Tung-p'o (1037–1101); he was a native of T'ai-p'ing-chou.

was young, Kung-fu composed some quite fine and unusual poetry and one of his elders declared approvingly that he must be a later day incarnation of Li Po.[20] When he was older, Kung-fu used to boast about this, and that was why Tung-p'o alluded to it as a joke.

14th day: The evening is clear and I opened the southern window and looked out at the mountains along the river. There are an amazing number of fish in the river. From time to time they break the surface of the water and come leaping up, catching the slanting rays of the sun and looking like silver knife blades. Everywhere you turn there are people fishing with lines or pulling in nets, and as a result the price of fish is extremely cheap. Every day the servants stuff themselves with it. The local people say that the river water is very rich and good for the fish. I tried drinking some and it does in fact have a sweet taste, though I find it hard to believe that the richness of the water accounts for the large number of fish. There are several peaks southeast of the river that look like lines of mascara—they are in fact the peaks of Green Mountains.

16th day: There was a gathering at the Taoist temple. I went around visiting the various pavilions and summer houses in the city. There is one called the Pavilion for Sitting and Whistling which provides an especially fine view from its upper story. The moats around the city are planted with lotus flowers. This evening the moonlight was as bright as day. The reflection of the moon in the river swayed and shimmered like a pagoda of white jade, and for the first time I understood the marvelous

20. According to Kuo's biography in *Sung shih* 444, the remark was made by the poet Mei Yao-ch'en (1002–1060).

skill of Su Tung-p'o's line, "The jade pagoda lies on the gentle waves." [21]

17th day: There was a gathering at the Li Po Shrine on Green Mountain; my two professor friends went along. The shrine is northwest of Green Mountain, about fifteen li from the mountain itself. Behind the shrine is the poet's grave, on a little hill that winds up and down and is actually an offshoot of the Green Mountain range. No one knows when the shrine was built. There is a stone pillar by the grave with an inscription by Liu Ch'üan-po of the T'ang, and from more recent times, a stele with an inscription by Chang Chen-fu which was set up when the shrine was repaired. Li Po wears a black head cloth, a white robe, and an embroidered jacket. At his side is another figure wearing a Taoist cap and a fur robe, offering him food—this represents Kuo Kung-fu.[22]

After an early meal, we went to Green Mountain. In a little market south of the mountain is the site of Hsieh Hsüan-hui's old home; [23] now a family named T'ang lives there. Looking south, there is nothing but level plain as far as the eye can reach. All around the house are flowing springs and unusual rocks, green woods and groves of speckled bamboo—truly a beautiful spot.

We climbed the mountain back of the house, following a steep and rugged trail for some three or four li. Then two Taoists appeared, offering us hot water to drink and inviting

21.   From the first of five poems entitled "River Moon" which Su wrote in the autumn of 1095.

22.   See p. 82, n. 19. After retiring from official life, Kuo lived on Green Mountain.

23.   Hsieh T'iao (464–499), a famous poet of late Six Dynasties times.

us to rest on the rocks under the pines. Another li farther on, we arrived at a hut where an old Taoist came out to greet us. Over seventy years old, his name is Chou and he is a native of Wei-chou. He's been living on this mountain for thirty years, but his cheeks are still the color of cinnabar and there is no trace of gray in his hair. There was also an old woman named Li who is eighty, though her sight and hearing are perfect and she laughs and chatters away without any sign of fatigue. She herself says that she has discovered the secret of the immortals.[24]

In front of the hut is a little pond called Lord Hsieh's Pond. The water tastes sweet and cold; even in the middle of summer, the pond never dries up. On the very top of the mountain is a little pavilion called, as you might expect, Lord Hsieh's Pavilion. As I gaze down at the mountains on four sides, they look like dragons slithering along, racing each other to get to the river valleys. The spot reminds me very much of Shun Mountain at home, except that the summit of Shun Mountain is very fertile and open—no different from a level plain. In this respect, this mountain can't compare to the one at home. Looking north from the pavilion, you face directly toward Li-yang. The old Taoist Chou says that when Wan-yen Liang came with his army of marauders, the sound of war drums shook the whole mountain range.[25]

24. On Lu Yu's interest in Taoist alchemy and the search for the elixir of immortality, see Ho Peng Yoke, Goh Thean Chye, and Beda Lim, *Lu Yu, the Poet-Alchemist*, Occasional Paper #13, Faculty of Asian Studies, the Australian National University, Canberra, 1972.

25. Wan-yen Liang was a member of the Chin ruling family who became emperor of the Chin in 1149 and in 1161 led an army south to invade the Sung; he was killed the same year.

By the time I got back to the boat in the evening, the first watch drum had already sounded. Professor Yang Hsin-po, who was among the company, told me that the grave of Huan Wen [26] is also located in the outskirts of the city. It is flanked by stone animals and horses of very fine workmanship, and there is also a stele that is carved with all sorts of representations of the carriages, horses, and costumes of the period. He says it is well worth seeing—I'm only sorry I can't make the trip.

18th day: In light rain we cast off the lines and moved out into the Ku-shu River and down into the Yangtze. Where the Ku-shu flows into the Yangtze, the clear and the muddy water flow side by side without becoming mixed. Having been pulled along the inlet for thirty li, we reached Ta-hsin Mouth, where we tied up the boat. From here we will go out into the big river. If we can get a following wind, then we can go on our way, though often we are held up for several days at a time by adverse winds and rain. There are two little mountains on either side of the mouth of the river called East Bridge and West Bridge; another name for them is Heaven Gate Mountains. At the water's edge there are lots of little boys selling water chestnuts, water lily seeds, and lotus seeds and root. At night I took a walk along the embankment to look at the moon.

20th day: About noon we untied the boat and passed Three Mountain Point. On top of the point there is a new shrine to the River Dragon. A Taoist, half drunk, was standing on the very edge of the sheer, moss-covered bank, watching the boats

26. Huan Wen (312–373) was a powerful military leader of the Eastern Chin dynasty.

go by—just to look at him was enough to make your heart turn cold with fear. He must be some kind of eccentric. In the river there were dozens of porpoises diving and surfacing, some black, some yellow. Suddenly a creature several feet long, bright red in color and shaped like a huge centipede, stuck up its head and swam upriver. It splashed water two or three feet into the air and was a really fearful sight. We spent the night at Kuo-tao Mouth.

23d day: We passed Sunny Mountain Point and for the first time caught sight of Mount Chiu-hua. The banks of the river are covered with reed blossoms—they look like snow. Once when I visited Yen-wei, the chief priest of the Temple of the Heavenly Well, he told me that the old monks of Mount Lu use the fluff from the reed blossoms to stuff their robes with. When Yen-wei was young and living at the Temple of the Compassionate Sun, he too made himself a robe of this kind, but when the Ch'an Master Fo-teng Hsün saw it, he gave Yen-wei a fierce scolding. "If at your age you're already so concerned about keeping warm, how can you put your mind to the study of the Dharma?" he said. When the interview was over, Yen-wei questioned the other monks and they told him that of the hundred men at the temple, no more than three or four had reed blossom robes, and they were all over seventy. At this he felt very embarrassed and quickly took off the robe.

We tied up at Plum Root Harbor.

26th day: We cast off the lines and passed Long Wind Sands and Raksha Stone. Li Po in his "Song of Ch'ang-kan" says:

If you are coming down through the narrows of the river
    Kiang
Please let me know beforehand

And I will come out to meet you
  As far as Cho-fu-sa (Long Wind Sands).[27]

It is seven hundred li from Chin-ling and yet the wife says she will come this far to greet her husband—the poet wishes to emphasize the great distance she is willing to go. The area is part of Shu-chou. In old times this section of the river was said to be extremely swift and dangerous, but in the reign of Emperor Jen-tsung (1023–1063), Chou Chan, who was charged with improving transportation, employed 300,000 workmen to open up a ten-li bypass in order to get around the worst part. To this day the boats that travel the river profit from his labors.

Raksha Stone is in the middle of the river, just like Peregrine Hill at Chen-chiang, only larger. The white rock rises up, with bushes and tall trees on its summit. You can also see the flag and pole of a small shrine, though I don't know what god it is dedicated to. To the west one can make out rows of mountains winding this way and that, rugged and craggy. They are very much like the mountains of Mirror Lake that I see when I look south from my house in Shao-hsing and make me sigh with longing. We spent the night at Huai Family Landing.

27th day: At the fifth watch drum, a strong wind began to blow from the northeast. Without informing me, the boatmen untied the boat and set out with the wind behind them. We passed Goose Wing Cove, where there is a tax office and about two hundred families. A great many boats were tied up at the bank. We went on past Wan Mouth till we reached

27. The translation is that of Ezra Pound, who entitles the poem "The River Merchant's Wife."

Chao Village—thus before the morning meal we had already gone 150 li, but the wind continued to increase in strength, so we tied up in a cove. There is a troop garrison at Chao Village as well as a small market place. The fierce wind continued all day and did not let up even at evening. I climbed the embankment and walked as far as the mouth of the cove, where I watched the huge waves leaping up from the river—even the eighth month tidal bore in the Ch'ien-t'ang River can't surpass this! There was a boat being blown about as though with a winnowing fan—it tried two or three times to enter the cove but couldn't make it, and seemed to be on the point of capsizing. It shouted for help, and only after a long time was finally able to reach the shore.

At night it rained.

28th day: We passed Tung-li District but did not stop at the town. From Thunder River Mouth we moved out into the big river. The rows of mountains on the south side of the river rise in layer after layer of brilliant green, lined up like screens for thirty or forty li without a break. We've seen nothing like this since we started west from Chin-ling. Today the wind is with us and we spread the sail. The boat moved along very fast, but the whole broad expanse of the river is covered with white waves like mountains and even the two thousand-bushel boat we are riding in rolls and bounces around as though it were a mere leaf.

We passed Lion Point, also called Buddha Finger Point. The mossy escarpment rises a hundred feet, with clumps of green trees and bushes growing out at all angles from the face of the cliff—it's more striking than a painting and I'm only sorry the boat was following the northern bank so we couldn't go directly beneath it. There are several points to the side of it which are also quite steep, though nothing like Lion Point.

We reached Ma-tang, where there is a shrine to the water god called Hsia-yüan shui-fu. The mountain rises up sheer and tall, the front of it projecting straight out into the river. The shrine is built right in the cliff, its hall suspended in the air, and anyone wanting to reach it must climb a narrow stony path that goes up the face of the cliff to the west of the hall, clinging to vines and feeling for a foothold, just as though he were climbing a ladder. The dipping rafters and zigzag railings of the hall shine vermilion and emerald in the distance. Of all the shrines along the river, this is the most beautiful.

As the boat reached the foot of the rocky cliff, the day suddenly grew dark and the wind came up with unexpected force. The boatmen's faces were filled with apprehension as they rushed to lower the sail and make for the small harbor. Working with all their might to pull the boat along, they were just barely able to get us into the harbor and make fast the mooring lines. There were four or five other boats tied up and they all came to help pull on the lines. One of the boats in this party is also headed for Shu. All at once a big fish, bright green with a patch of red the color of cinnabar on its belly, came leaping out of the water beside the rudder, rising some three feet into the air. We were all very startled.

This evening, as we had feared, the mast broke and the sail was so badly damaged it can hardly be used—another ominous occurrence. When night came, the wind blew stronger than ever and we had to put out more than ten extra mooring lines. Only with the dawn did it begin to subside a little.

29th day: Held up by wind in Ma-tang Harbor. The wind and rain are cold and biting and for the first time I've had to put on a lined robe. Some little boats came, braving the wind and waves, selling firewood, vegetables, and pork. One of them was also selling wild boar meat—someone out hunting had killed a boar in a field of rushes, we were told.

After eating, I climbed up on the embankment to the south and looked at the Ma-tang shrine in the distance. The north wind was blowing so strong that one couldn't even talk in the face of it. Toward evening it began to die down a little, but the angry waves had not yet subsided and I could hear them slapping against the boat all night long.

8th month, 2d day: Got an early start, but before we'd gone twenty li a strong wind suddenly started to blow and clouds raced across the sky. We rushed to tie up but then, just as abruptly as it had clouded over, it cleared and we went on our way again, floating past the mouth of Lake P'eng-li. From the mouth of the lake a tributary enters the main river—called the Nan-chiang (Southern Yangtze), it provides access to the region of Chiang-hsi. The water of the main river is muddy and turgid, and whenever you want to use it, you have to put apricot kernels in it first to purify it and then let it stand overnight before it's fit to drink. The Nan-chiang, on the other hand, is extremely clear and pure, and where the rivers come together, their waters flow side by side like two strands of rope, never mixing. At night we reached Chiang-chou (Kiukiang) and tied up at P'en Bank. The water is very clear, not contaminated with that of the main river. From the 26th of last month to today is six days, but one day we were held up by wind and couldn't proceed, so in fact we have been traveling upstream for four and a half days. In that time we've gone seven hundred li.

4th day: On an outing to the Taoist Temple of Heavenly Blessing. I met the head of the temple Li Shou-chih and asked him about the jade fungus of immortality, but he was unable to give me any answer. The buildings of the temple are all very old and though they escaped being burned by soldiers, what is left of them has fallen into ruin. The only thing to see is the statue of Lao Tzu in the Hall of Great Purity. It is a clay image dating from the T'ang—very old and wonderful. There are also statues of men and women immortals, officials of the other world, guardians, and boy attendants, two of each. In addition, there is a gilded bronze figure of Emperor Hsüan-tsung of the T'ang wearing robes and cap like those of a Taoist and looking very solemn and righteous—exactly the air of one who has reigned for fifty years and enjoyed all the wealth and eminence of an era of perfect peace.[28] Li Shou-chih is a native of Lai-an in Ch'u-chou. He says that his family was originally wealthy and prosperous but when the troubles came, he left home and became a Taoist. General Yüeh Fei[29] was the one who conferred upon him the certificate making him an official member of the Taoist clergy, and to this day he keeps a portrait of the general and his son to which he pays obeisance.

Shih Chih-tao, a local official, invited me to drink at the Transport Office. We climbed the High Distant Pavilion and looked at Mount Lu. The weather was very clear and we

28. There is a note of irony in Lu Yu's remark. Emperor Hsüan-tsung, who came to the throne in 713, did enjoy several decades of peace and prosperity, but in 755 was driven from the capital by the An Lu-shan rebellion and forced to abdicate in favor of his son. The T'ang emperors were enthusiastic patrons of Taoism.

29. 1103–1141, a general who distinguished himself in attacks on the Chin invaders. He rose to a position of great eminence but, the victim of jealousy and opposition from the peace party, was imprisoned and put to death in 1141.

could see all the various peaks of the mountain. Chih-tao brought out some of the new iron cash that have just been minted.

6th day: Around eight in the evening, several hundred large round lanterns came floating out from P'en Bank, covering the surface of the water and drifting downstream. When they reached the wide part of the river, they spread out and gradually went off into the distance, shining beautifully like so many stars in the sky. The local people tell me that each family releases five hundred lanterns in order to drive off calamity and pray for good fortune. It's an old custom in this stretch of the river, they say.

7th day: I went to Mount Lu, stopping for a short rest at New Bridge Market. It is on the main road between the regions of Wu and Shu and I saw the names of many Shu people written on the walls of the shops in the market. There are tall trees here and there along both sides of the river, all of them two or three hundred years old—the place is actually part of the foothills of the mountain. From Chiang-chou to the Hall of Great Peace and National Prosperity is a distance of thirty li, and this is exactly halfway in between. Today the carriages and horses and people on foot went streaming by me without a break. "Climbing up to the Taoist Temple," they call it— that is, going to burn incense at the Great Peace Hall. This goes on from the 1st day of the 8th month until the 7th day and is called the White Lotus Gathering. The White Lotus Society was originally founded by the Buddhist priest Hui-yüan,[30] but there is an old legend that he once agreed to lend

30. 334–416, an eminent Buddhist monk and scholar who founded the Tung-lin-ssu or Temple of the Eastern Forest on Mt.

his White Lotus to the Taoists for one day, and ever since then it has been the custom to hold such a gathering each year at the Great Peace Hall. The Buddhist Temple of the Eastern Forest also has its own gathering but, contrary to what you might expect, fewer people attend it than attend the one at Great Peace Hall, which is rather ironical.

In the evening I reached the Clear Void Retreat, situated at the foot of the Peak that Scatters the Clouds. This is where the Taoist Priest Huang-fu resides. Huang-fu's name is T'an and he is a native of Chia-chou. At the moment he is away, traveling through the nearby districts, and I was only able to see his disciple Ts'ao Mi-shen. I spent the night in the west room of the retreat. Young Ts'ao brought wine to the room and broiled some venison which was very tasty. The wine was extremely clear and pure. At night it was cold enough to make one welcome a fire.

10th day: In the evening I said good-by to my various friends. For several nights in a row I've been staying in the mountains where it is very cold and one has to have a fire going, but now I'm back on the boat I find that the autumn heat has not yet ended—I'm fanning myself all day long.

11th day: We cast off the lines and started on our way. It has been ten days since we reached Chiang-chou and the weather has been good the whole time. The air is clear and the autumn sky stretches far off without a trace of cloud—just right for climbing high places and enjoying the view, and also the kind of weather that travelers are thankful for. We tied up at the mouth of Red Sand Lake. Off to the northeast, we can still see Mount Lu.

Lu and organized the White Lotus Society, a group of monks and laymen who met to pay devotion to the Buddha Amida.

12th day: In the middle of the river, looking at the sights, among them a fish with two horns which from a distance looked just like a small calf. It would surface and then dive again, making a noise. In the evening we tied up at Lu-ch'i Landing. In the tall mountains on the other side of the river we could see two points of fire like lamps that for a long time blinked on and off. I asked the boatmen what they were but none of them knew. Some thought they were the eyes of a dragon, others that they were the glow from some magic fungus or immortality pill. There's no way to find out for certain.

13th day: We reached the Chao-yung Shrine at Rich Pond. Carrying a jar of wine and a sacrificial pig, I went to pay my respects to the deity, the "Brilliant Martial Beloved Efficacious Prince." The deity is Kan Hsing-pa (Kan Ning), who served as a general under the Great Emperor of the Wu.[31] Hsing-pa was once governor of Hsi-ling and therefore his shrine is situated here. In the *k'ai-pao* era (968–976), after the region south of the Yangtze had been brought under control, the various deities in the shrines along the Yangtze and Huai rivers were enfeoffed with additional titles.[32] Thus Hsing-pa became the "Duke Who Protects the Nation." During the *hsüan-ho* era (1119–1125), his rank was raised to that of prince. In the *chien-yen* era (1127–1130), the powerful bandit leader Chang Yü, nicknamed the Hornets' Nest, visited the shrine with his band of soldiers. The men all began tossing shells to

31. Sun Ch'üan (182–252), founder of the state of Wu, one of the Three Kingdoms; see p. 76 n. 12.

32. It was assumed that the deities had helped the Sung armies to victory and they were therefore rewarded by the government with various honorary titles.

determine their fortune,[33] but one of the shells flew up into the air and remained suspended there, while the other one went leaping out the door. Terrified, the robbers withdrew from the place, and not long afterwards, they were wiped out. General Liu Kuang-shih reported the incident to the throne, and the emperor ordered further titles to be bestowed on the god. When Yüeh Fei became *hsüan-fu-shih* (1137), he had extensive repairs made to the shrine. None of the shrines along the river cam compare to it. The god's consort is enfeoffed as Lady Obedient Protectress, his two sons as the marquises Bright Awe and Bright Holiness, and his daughter as Lady Gentle Virtue. There are statues of all of them, as well as seated statues of the prince and his consort in another hall behind the main one. Day and night people come to make offerings at the shrine, and the head of the shrine receives a yearly stipend of 1,200 strings of cash from the government—from this one can judge how great is the deity's power. The boatmen tell me that if one prays to him with all one's might, he will divide the winds and give a favorable wind to each boat, whether it is going upriver or down. On the porch of the shrine is a statue of Kuan Yün-ch'ang.[34] Kuan Yün-ch'ang ought not to be worshiped in a shrine dedicated to Kan Hsing-pa, since the two men were loyal to different masters. For the two deities to receive sacrifices side by side can't help but be an embarrassment to both of them.

33. River mussel shells, or pieces of wood or bamboo shaped like shells, were cast and the fortune told on the basis of whether they fell face up or face down.

34. Kuan Yü (d. 219), general of the kingdom of Shu in the Three Kingdoms period and hence an enemy of the ruler of Wu and his general Kan Hsing-pa.

After presenting my offering, I walked up behind the shrine to the Temple of Manifest Teaching. The temple is being used as a wine tax and wine control office. The statues and other fixtures are put away in one little room and the monks have all been driven off. What a way to do things!

14th day: It rained at dawn. Moving out into the big river, we met a raft made of wood and measuring over ten or more chang across and over fifty chang long. There were thirty or forty houses on it, complete with wives and children, chickens and dogs, mortars and pestles. Little paths ran back and forth and there was even a shrine—I've never seen anything like it. The boatmen tell me that this is actually a rather small raft. The big ones sometimes have soil spread over the surface and vegetable gardens planted, or wine shops built on them. They are unable to enter the coves but travel only on the big river.

Today we had the wind against us and the boat had to be pulled along. From dawn to sunset we barely managed to go fifteen or sixteen li. We tied up at the side of Liu-kuan Point. We have reached the border of Ch'i-chou. The boys went ashore, and when they got back, they said they had found a little path that led around behind the mountains, where they came upon a man-made lake, very wide, with many lotuses and water chestnuts. There were numerous water mallows growing along the bank. Several houses basked in the late sun, with rush hedges and thatched roofs—truly a rare and picturesque spot, yet lonely and with no sound of human voices. They saw some large pears which they wanted to buy, but could find no one to buy them from. There was a little boat out on the lake gathering water chestnuts which they called to, but got no answer. They were about to press on farther when they saw some traps at the side of the road and, fearing that there might be tigers or wolves around, they didn't dare go on.

In the evening we saw a big turtle bobbing up and down in the water.

15th day: Somewhat overcast. The west wind is getting stronger and it is extremely difficult to tow the boat. From Rich Pond west we've been following the south bank of the river—nothing but big mountains rising and dipping like billows. There are people living here and there at the foot of the mountains. From time to time we see them crouching in sheds they've made, holding bows and arrows and watching for a tiger to go by. We passed Dragon's Eye Point, a mere fist of stone in the river. On the mountain beside the point there is a dragon shrine. Sometime after four in the afternoon, the wind shifted around behind us. We stopped for the night at Ch'i Mouth Garrison, where there are many houses crowded together and a large number of boats bound for Shu tied up at the embankment.

In the evening I climbed up on the bank with my sons and looked out over the great river, enjoying the moonlight. The surface of the river stretches far off to the horizon and the reflection of the moon falls across the water, rippling and swaying and never coming to rest, like a golden dragon—a sight to amaze the eye and move the heart.

Today I bought prepared medicine at the Ch'i Mouth market. In the medicine shops are all the things one needs for simmering and decocting such as peppermint and black plum preparation. Such ingredients are hard to get hold of suddenly when one is on a journey—that the medicine shops were thoughtful enough to stock them is very commendable.

18th day: We finally got started at mealtime and by four in the afternoon reached Huang-chou. It is an out-of-the-way and backward place where there is little to do. But because Tu Mu and Wang Yü-ch'eng [35] were once its governors and Su Tung-p'o and Chang Lei [36] lived here in exile, it has ended by becoming a famous town. We tied up at the Lin-kao Pavilion, where Su Tung-p'o once stayed, the place of which he said in a letter to Ch'in Shao-yu,[37] "a few steps out the gate and you are at the great river." The misty waves stretch far into the distance and the spot has an open and spacious air.

I called on the governor Yang Yu-i and the vice-governor Ch'en Shao-fu. The governor's office is extremely shabby—the reception room barely holds four or five visitors—though the building his assistants are in is somewhat better.

In the evening we shifted the boat to Bamboo Garden Port. There was too much wind and rough water at Lin-kao—it's no place to tie up for the night.

21st day: We passed Twin Willow Cove. Looking back over the river, we could see distant mountains piled on top of each other, jagged and steep. Since leaving Huang-chou, we've been going through a series of coves, but all of them broad and open. The land along the river is gradually getting higher and is planted mostly in crops such as beans, millet, and buckwheat. In the evening we tied up at Willow Row Landing—a big embankment with tall willows and many people living crowded together. Fish are as cheap as dirt—a hundred cash will buy enough to satisfy twenty mouths. What's more, they're all large fish. I tried to find some small fish to feed to my cat but couldn't.

35. Tu Mu (803–852) was a famous T'ang poet-official, Wang Yü-ch'eng (954–1001) a poet-official of the Northern Sung.

36. On Su Tung-p'o and Chang Lei, see nn. 18–19, pp. 81–82.

37. Ch'in Kuan (1049–1101), disciple of Su Tung-p'o.

23d day: The wind with us, we spread the sail. This is the first time we've had a favorable wind since the 14th. At meal-time we reached O-chou (Wu-ch'ang) and tied up at the tax pavilion. There are countless boats belonging to peddlers and travelers tied up bow to stern in an unbroken line for several li. We've seen nothing like this west of Chen-chiang. The city is very large and prosperous, with rows of shops packed together, and beyond the city wall to the south there is also a market extending for several li. Even Ch'ien-t'ang (Hangchow) and Chien-k'ang (Nanking) can't surpass it—it is, in fact, a major metropolis. From Chiang-chou (Kiukiang) to this place is a journey of seven hundred li, traveling upriver against the current, and even if you had a favorable wind every day, it would still take three or four days. When Han Yü said, "With the wind behind you, you can go from P'en-ch'eng (Kiukiang) to O-chou in no more than a day," he was quite mistaken.[38] Obviously he had never made the trip.

25th day: I watched the troops staging a mock battle on the water. There were seven hundred large warships, each twenty or thirty chang long and fitted out with walls and turrets. Their flags and pennants shone brightly, their gongs and drums clattered and clanged as they raced back and forth, crashing through the huge waves as swiftly as though they had wings. Thirty or forty thousand people came to watch —it was in fact one of the most spectacular sights in the world.

29th day: Early in the morning a priest from Kuang-han named Shih-ch'üan and one from Tso-mien named Liao-cheng

38. Han Yü (768–824), the famous T'ang Confucian scholar, poet, and prose stylist. The quotation is from a poem written by Han Yü at Chiang-chou and sent to a Lord Li of O-yueh.

came to call—they will be coming along in our boat as passengers. At sunset we shifted the boat to River Mouth. Looking back at the embankment, we could see a great jumble of tall buildings and towers where lamps were burning and people were singing and shouting—it was midnight before they quieted down.

I sent for a doctor named Chao Sui to examine Ling-chao.[39]

30th day: At dawn we left O-chou and, with the wind behind us, hoisted sail and followed Parrot Shoals, traveling south. Above the shoals is a dense forest and a shrine—from a distance it looks like Small Mountain. This is the place where Ni Heng was put to death.[40] From here on south is the Han River.[41] The water is clear and bright as a mirror. We passed Hsieh Family Point and Golden Rooster Landing. The point is not very high; the rocks are all split horizontally and look like layers of tile piled up. We bought shrunk-necked carp that weighed ten catties. At the landing there is a large community—almost like a small district town. The region produces sturgeon and the families in the community all make a living by selling pickled fish. At evening we tied up at T'ung-chi Mouth. From here we enter the bypass. After the ninth month, the water in the bypass dries up and it becomes impassable—one has to go around by way of Pa-ling to get to Ching-chou.

39. A servant? The name indicates only that it is a woman.

40. A poet and writer of the late 2d cen. A.D., famous for his unconventional behavior. He finally outraged his patron to such an extent that he was put to death.

41. I do not understand this statement. At this point the course of the Yangtze runs approximately north and south, and the Han River enters it from the west.

9th month, 1st day: We entered the bypass, which is in reality a small tributary of the Yangtze. We passed New Deeps, where there is a dragon shrine, very beautiful and well kept. From here on there are no more houses. Both banks are covered with reeds and rushes as far as one can see—the place is called Hundred Li Wasteland. In addition there is no path for the towmen, so the boatmen had to put out little boats to pull on the "hundred-chang" towing lines.[42] By nighttime we had gone barely 45 li. We tied up among the clumps of reeds. People traveling through here by boat are very likely to encounter bandits and therefore the inspector of T'ung-chi patrols the area with armed men. I didn't get to sleep until dawn.

2d day: The reeds on the east bank are becoming a little thinner and there are occasional breaks through which we can see the big river stretching far off—that is the way to Pa-ling. At sunset we stopped for the night at Hsia-chün. We began to see houses again, some twenty families or more, all making their living at fishing. With rush hedges and thatched roofs, the houses make a very picturesque sight. Fish are so cheap they can hardly be said to cost anything at all. From here the towpath begins again. I climbed up onto the roof of the boat and looked at the distant mountains of Ching-ling. We tied up at White Mortar where there are several farm families living. Outside each gate are old willows reaching up to the clouds.

3d day: From the time we entered the bypass we have had no vegetables to eat, but today for the first time we got some greens and turnips. The people were unwilling to give us the roots as well, however, but merely cut off some of the leaves. We passed Eight Fold Landing Mouth where there are also

42. On the "hundred-chang" towing lines, see p. 105.

people living. At evening we tied up at Kuei-tzu Fort. There are over ten families living here as well and many mulberries, paper mulberries, elms, and willows.

4th day: It was dawn before we got under way. The boatmen tell me that from here on along the bank there are many dikes and ponds where the grass is thick and overgrown and tigers and wolves prowl about. If we start out before it gets light, many of the towmen are likely to be injured.

We passed Net Port, where there are twenty or more houses. Set among tall willows in the late sun, with nets spread out to dry on their low hedges and little boats going back and forth in front of them, they looked just like something out of a painting. This is the prettiest place on the bypass. We tied up at Pi Family Pond. The land around here is high and hilly, with quite a number of people living on it. There were one or two houses which, although they were hardly more than cottages thatched with reeds, had very trim and well-constructed doors and windows and sturdy fences around them, and to the side were beautiful groves of fruit trees—they were the most impressive houses in the whole village.

I went ashore with the boys and the two monks and we visited the Temple of Fortune Everlasting, a silent, deserted place with no one around. In front of the White Cloud Chapel, on the east side of the temple, was an orange tree just now bearing fruit, rather small but extremely fragrant. We took turns making tea for each other and squeezed some of the oranges into the tea. At nightfall we went back to the boat.

6th day: Passed East Ground. The water is flanked on both sides by dense bamboo and groves of tall trees and the embankment is so clean it looks as though it's been swept. Chickens and dogs wander leisurely about, wild and domestic ducks bob up and down on the water, and people pass back and forth in the shade of the trees, or at times come down to the ferry landing and call for a boat—it makes you feel quite enraptured, as though you had stumbled upon a different world. The boatmen tell me that this whole area is part of an estate belonging to a rich family of the village. We tied up at Chicken Crow.

8th day: In the morning we stopped at Chien-ning Garrison in Chiang-ling, which is at the mouth of the bypass, because the wind was against us. There are countless large fish swimming in the water. We have been traveling through the bypass for seven days—from here we move out into the Yangtze River and enter the territory of Shih-shou District. At night we watched them burning the reeds on the other side of the river. The smoke and flames reached up to the sky—it looked like a city wall lined with torches. The glow from it lit up our boat and turned everything red.

9th day: Early in the morning I paid my respects at the shrine of the Earth Lord. The thatched roofs on the houses along the road are all a foot in thickness, neatly trimmed and without a single stalk out of place.

We raised the sail and set out on the river, traveling thirty li and tying up at Pagoda Point, a large mountain on the edge of the river. This is the first time we've seen any mountains since leaving O-chou. We bought some mutton and set out wine. In honor of Double-ninth,[43] the people in the riverside village had slaughtered a sheep and the various boats began buying the meat until in no time it was all gone. I went looking for

43. The ninth day of the ninth lunar month, when it was customary to gather with friends, especially in some high place, and drink wine with chrysanthemum blossoms floating in it.

chrysanthemum flowers at the houses along the river and managed to get several sprays, very fragrant and attractive. With that, I felt quite satisfied and proceeded to get drunk. The rain at night was very cold and for the first time I used a wadded quilt.

10th day: Held up by adverse wind, we sent a little boat across the river to the other bank to buy some meat. The party came back with half of a large fish, along with a rooster, which we can't bear to kill and are keeping on the boat. An old man from the village suddenly appeared with a present of water parsley shoots, for which he refused to accept any payment. We sent a man ahead to K'uei. At evening it cleared and I opened the window of the boat and looked out at the moon.

13th day: We tied up at Willow Boy. At night I visited on the boat with the priests Shih-ch'üan and Liao-cheng and listened to them chanting the *Heart Sutra* in Sanskrit. Only the priests of Shu know how to chant this sutra.

17th day: After sundown we shifted our baggage to a boat belonging to Chao Ch'ing of Chia-chou—the kind used for traveling through the gorges. Most of the people living along the embankment of Sand Market are natives of Shu or are married to people from Shu.

20th day: We have taken down the mast and prepared the fixtures for the oars. Going up the gorges, we will use only oars and "hundred-chang" towing lines and will not spread the sail. The "hundred-chang" are made of huge pieces of bamboo split into four strands and are as big around as a man's arm. The boat I'm riding on, of the 1,600-bushel class, uses six oars and two hundred-chang lines wound on winches.

27th day: We untied the boat, beat the drum, and rattled the oars, the boatmen all making a great clamor. There was a veritable wall of people lined up on the embankment to watch. We tied up at New River Mouth, which is three or four li from Sand Market; it is the place where the men of Shu repair their boats.

28th day: We tied up at Fang-ch'eng. There is a man named Wang Po-i from Chia-chou who earlier, in response to our request, agreed to act as *chao-t'ou* or chief helmsman of the boat; he was given special pay, and whenever an offering of meat was made to the gods, he received twice as much as the other men. Chao Ch'ing, the owner of the boat, decided to get rid of Wang and instead employ Ch'eng Hsiao-pa, a favorite of his, as chief helmsman. Wang, having lost his job, was very downcast but couldn't bring himself to leave the boat entirely. Finally he went out of his head and jumped into the water. I hurriedly sent men to try to save him, and after he had drifted downriver for over a li and had gone down and come up three times, they barely succeeded in fishing him out. If merely losing one's assignment as chief helmsman can make a man try to kill himself, what would a more serious loss do?

29th day: Held up by adverse wind.

10th month, 1st day: We passed Kua-chou Incline, Granary Head, and Hundred Li Beach, tying up at T'o-yung. There are settlements at each of these places with groves of dense bamboo and houses within sight of each other. We also saw a village schoolmaster in the midst of giving a lesson to his pupils. When the boys spotted the boat going by, they all tucked their school books under their arms and came out to watch, some of them still continuing to recite their lesson. "T'o" is another name for the Yangtze, mentioned in the *Odes*—"On the Yangtze is the T'o" [44]—and in the "Tribute of Yü"— "Min Mountains lead the Yangtze east to become the T'o." [45] "Yung" is defined by the *Erh ya* as a river which has water in it in spring, summer, and fall, but none in the winter.

2d day: We tied up at Cassia Forest Bay. The priests Shih-ch'üan and Liao-cheng have been traveling by land and they say that most of the people living along the road are from some other part of the country—not more than one in ten is a native of this region. The boatmen killed over ten pigs and made a sacrifice to the gods—they called it a "starter."

8th day: When the fifth watch drum had finished sounding, we cast off and passed Hsia-lao Pass. Flanking the river on either side are a thousand peaks and ten thousand pinnacles, some shoving up in clusters, some soaring alone, some so cracked they seem about to shatter, some so steep they seem about to fall, some split crosswise, some cleft straight down, some with knobs sticking out, some with hollows, some with cracks—strange and eerie shapes that one could never finish describing. Since winter has just begun, the grass and trees are still green and unwithered. Looking off to the west, one sees mountains piled up like a gateway from which the river emerges—this is what is called Hsia-lao Valley.

We tied up the boat and the boys, the priest Liao-cheng, and I climbed up to the Grotto of the Three Wanderers. We made our way up a path cut in the stone for two li, the slope so steep we could hardly get a footing. The grotto is the size

44. *Odes*, Mao #22.

45. The "Tribute of Yü" or Yü-kung is a section of the *Shu ching* or *Book of Documents*.

of a three room house. There is a tunnel leading to it, big enough for a person to get through, though dark and steep and very frightening. Or one can wind back and forth across the face of the mountain, crouching and crawling up from the base of the cliff to the front of the grotto. This is perhaps a little easier, and yet one looks right down into the deep water in the valley, the rocky wall is over ten chang in height, and the sound of the water is terrifying.[46] There is another tunnel, this one with a wall at the end, which could be used as a dwelling. There are stalactites so old that they reach all the way to the ground and look like pillars.

We tied up at Stone Tablet Gorge. There is a cave in the rock with a stone in it that is shaped exactly like an old man holding a fishing pole.

9th day: Light breeze. We passed Swinging Door Gorge. The mountains on either side seem about to come together like the leaves of a swinging door, and I suspect that is where the name came from. I climbed up to Toad Hillock. The spring here is listed in fourth place in the "Classification of Waters." [47] The "Toad" is at the foot of the mountain, overlooking the river. His head, nose, lips, and chin are all very realistic, but most lifelike of all are the bumps on the skin of his back—to think that the Creator could display such skill!

46. I am not certain I have understood this description of the approach to the grotto correctly. The poem which Lu Yu wrote describing his visit (CNSK 2) makes it clear that he approached the grotto through a dark and frightening tunnel. The grotto derives its name from a visit paid to it by the T'ang poet Po Chü-i (772–846), his younger brother Hsing-chien, and his close friend Yüan Chen.

47. In the second list in the *Chien-ch'a shui-chi*.

Going inland a way from the toad's back, one comes to a cave where the rocks are green and shiny. A spring, clear and cold and making a rippling noise, flows out of the cave and falls down over the nose and mouth of the toad, forming a curtain of water that descends to the river. Today was very cold and there was snow piled on the mountain peaks, and yet inside the cave it was as warm as spring. Opposite the hillock and the cave, a little to the west, is a peak which rises up all alone among the clouds, called the Peak of the Pillar of Heaven. From here on, the mountains become a little less rugged, but the banks of the river are covered with big boulders heaped about everywhere one looks, as though someone had dug a channel and piled up the dirt on either side.

In the evening we stopped at the shrine at Yellow Ox, where the mountains again become steep and high. A great many villagers came selling tea and vegetables. Among them were some women, all wearing green patterned kerchiefs wrapped around their heads—they were fair in complexion and their speech was very correct. The tea, on the other hand, resembled twigs of brushwood or leaves of grass, and was so bitter you couldn't put it in your mouth.

The shrine is called the Shrine of Magic Response and the god is enfeoffed as the Marquis Who Responds and Protects; both names were bestowed by imperial decree in the *shao-hsing* era (1131–1162) or after. Below the shrine are the Unrighteous Rapids, where a jumble of boulders blocks the current. Looking down on it, it appears terrifying, and yet when we passed through it in the boat, I didn't feel particularly disturbed, so skillfully did the boatmen do their work. Legend says that the god of the shrine assisted Emperor Yü of the Hsia in fixing the course of the rivers, and in recognition of his effort, he is worshiped here.[48] There are stone horses to the left and right of the gate, one on each side, rather small, with a little roof over each one. The horse on the right is missing its left ear—these are the ones that Ou-yang Hsiu saw.[49] Behind the shrine is a grove of trees that look like ilex but are not—no one could tell me the name of them. The fallen leaves have black markings on them like the characters on an amulet and no two leaves are alike. The boys gathered up a number of the leaves. There is a stone engraved with a poem by Ou-yang Hsiu.

At night the boatmen came to ask if it would be all right not to sound the watch drums. They said there are many tigers in the mountains behind the shrine which come out if they hear the drums.

10th day: Early in the morning I took a sacrificial pig and a jar of wine and offered them at the Shrine of Magic Response and then we got under way, passing through the Deer Horn, Tiger Head, and Shih-chün rapids. The water has already fallen to two thirds of its maximum height and yet the swift current is dangerous enough to fill one with terror. We tied up at a place called Below-the-Castle, on the border of the Tzu-kuei District of Kuei-chou. I went for a walk along the

48. Emperor Yü is a legendary ruler of high antiquity who rescued China from flood by opening up courses for the Yangtze and other rivers and leading them east to the sea.

49. Ou-yang Hsiu (1007–1072), famous Sung scholar and statesman. In 1036 he was exiled to Yi-ling, at the mouth of the Yangtze gorges, and the following year wrote a poem describing his visit to the shrine at Yellow Ox and mentioning the stone horses. It was this poem which was engraved on the stone mentioned a few sentences below.

sand with the boys. Turning around, we could look straight back at Yellow Ox Gorge, where the mountains behind the shrine rise up steeply to the sky like rows and rows of screens. On top of the fourth row is something shaped like an ox, reddish-yellow in color, with what looks like a man wearing a cap standing in front of it. Yesterday and this morning there were clouds hiding the tops of the mountains, so this is the first time we've been able to see it.

We walked on to the Temple of Merciful Salvation in White Sand Market and called on the chief priest Chih-chien. I asked him how the place came to be called Below-the-Castle, and he said that back of the temple there was an old castle, still in existence, which dated from the days of the Ch'u kingdom.[50] We all proceeded to go visit it. It is on a hill, very small, with gates on the north and south, and overlooks the river opposite Yellow Ox Gorge. Northwest of the castle is a mountain that winds around and turns back on itself, and on top of it, a shrine to Wu Tzu-hsü.[51] On the whole, there are a great many Wu Tzu-hsü shrines west of Ching. Below the castle are many beautiful rocks like those of Ling-pi and Hu-k'ou.

11th day: We passed Open Grotto Rapids. The rapids are very dangerous and so I put my family in sedan chairs and we made our way around them by land. There are many strange rocks along the edge of the rapids, sparkling with all the five colors and delighting the eye. Some have markings on them that look like various objects or the writing on an amulet. We can still see the mountains behind the shrine at Yellow Ox Gorge.

50. See the poem on p. 5.

51. See p. 52, n. 1.

In the evening we tied up at the mouth of Horse Liver Gorge, where two mountains stand face to face, their tall crests scraping against the sky—they look rather like Mount Lu. There are many boulders along the edge of the river and the hundred-chang towing lines keep getting tangled around them, making it very difficult to proceed. At night we had a little rain.

13th day: The boat started up New Rapids, following the south bank, but when it had gone about seven or eight tenths of the way, the bottom was smashed by a rock. I sent men to the rescue and we somehow managed to keep it from sinking, but a sharp rock was poking right through the bottom and the boat was stuck fast and wouldn't move. This happened because the boatmen have loaded us down with a cargo of pottery. Of the two banks of New Rapids, the southern one is called Government Watercourse and the northern one Dragon Gate. The current on the Dragon Gate side is very swift and there are many hidden rocks. The Government Watercourse side is a little easier to travel along, though there are also many sharp rocks—this is why this is the most dangerous spot in the gorges. Unless one removes all cargo and makes the boat as light as possible, one can't go up or down. But the boatmen in their eagerness to turn a profit have ended up like this—let it serve as a warning!

I visited the North Shrine on the river bank. The shrine overlooks Dragon Gate and below it, in a cleft in the rock, there is a hot spring. It is shallow but never dries up, and the whole village depends on it. The women come to dip up water, all carrying on their backs jars hollowed out of a single piece of wood, two feet long, with three little feet on the bottom. When they get to the side of the spring, they dip up the water with a dipper and when the jar is eight tenths full, they sit down beside the rock on which the jar is resting, tie the jar to their backs, and go off with it. On the whole the people in the gorges carry everything on their backs. There are many women, and they carry not only water but wine on their backs as well, which they peddle. They carry it in the same fashion as the water, and when you ask them to sell you some, they kneel down very politely and present it to you. The unmarried ones all wear their hair in a "paired-heart" hairdo, two feet high, with as many as six silver hairpins stuck in it. Behind the hairpins they also stick a large ivory comb as big as a hand.

15th day: The boatmen unloaded all the cargo and were finally able to pull the boat past the rapids, but it will have to be repaired, so we have shifted to another boat. We left New Rapids, passed through White Dog Gorge, and tied up at Hsing Mountain Mouth. I went by sedan chair to visit the Grotto of the Jade Void, which is about five li from the river bank. It is on the other side of a small river, called Fragrant River, which has its origin in Chao-chün Village.[52] The water has a very fine flavor; it is listed in the "Classification of Waters" and is green in color like mascara. I hailed a little boat, had myself ferried across the river, and proceeded on for a li or so more. The entrance to the grotto is small—barely one chang across—but once you are inside, it is extremely large —big enough to hold several hundred people—and so spacious and grand that you think you have entered the great hall of a palace. There are stones shaped like streamers and flags,

52. Said to be the birthplace of Wang Chao-chün, a court lady of the first cen. B.C., who was sent off to be the bride of the chief of the Hsiung-nu, a nomadic people living in the Gobi desert area. She is frequently depicted in Chinese art and literature.

fungus plants and bamboo shoots, immortals, dragons, tigers, birds, and beasts—a thousand shapes, ten thousand forms, each looking exactly like the real thing. Most astonishing of all are a circular stone on the east side that resembles the sun, and a semicircular stone on the west that resembles the moon. Of all the caves I've seen in my life, there's nothing to match it! There is a plaque inscribed by Hsieh Shih-hou and Ts'en Yen-ch'i in the *hsi-ning* era (1068–1077), and an inscription by Ch'en Yao-tzu relating the history of the grotto. It says that the grotto was first discovered by a hunter in the *t'ien-pao* era (742–755) of the T'ang. By the time I got ready to go home, night had already fallen and the wind was so strong that I couldn't use a candle, but the full moon shone as bright as day. The boys and the priest Shih-ch'üan carried walking sticks and followed along after me and we were hardly conscious of the steepness of the cliffs and valleys.

16th day: We reached Kuei-chou and I called on the governor Chia Hsüan and the vice governor Ch'en Tuan-yen. I found lodging at the Temple of Gratitude and Filial Piety, about a li from the town, a lonely place with no priest in residence. Though Kuei-chou is the capital of Kuei Province, it has barely three or four hundred families. It overlooks the river, with Sleeping Ox Mountain at its back, and there is not a foot of level ground in the whole town. The noise of the rapids never ceases, like a violent wind and rain storm about to descend.

On the opposite side of the river is the Castle of the King of Ch'u, also in a mountainous valley, though the ground is a little more level than at Kuei-chou. Some say that this is where the rulers of Ch'u were first enfeoffed. The *Classic of Mountains and Seas* says: "Ch'i of the Hsia dynasty enfeoffed Meng

Ch'u at Tan-yang Castle," and Kuo P'u's note on this asserts that Tan-yang is located south of Tzu-kuei District, so one might suppose that this was the spot. On the other hand, the *Records of the Historian* says: "King Ch'eng enfeoffed Hsiung Yi at Tan-yang," and P'ei Yin's commentary says that Tan-yang is in Chih River District.[53] So I can't tell which is correct.

18th day: Finally managed to get a boat of the kind called a *ch'an.* It is rather small, but light and with a broad bottom—well suited for ascending the rapids.

19th day: Went to a gathering at the Hall of the Homeland Return. I had hoped to get started this evening but it proved impossible. I visited the house of Sung Yü,[54] situated east of the district town of Tzu-kuei; it now belongs to a family of wine sellers. In old times there was a stone with the words "Sung Yü's House" carved on it, but because one of the words coincided with a tabooed name in the governor's family, the people of the province removed it. As a result, I'm afraid in time everyone will forget whose house it was, which would be a great pity.

21st day: From the boat I looked at Stone Gate Pass in the distance. It is barely wide enough for one person to get through; if manned, it must be the most impregnable spot in the world. In the evening we tied up at Pa-tung District. The mountains and the river at this point are majestic and beauti-

53. The statements are found in *Shan-hai-ching*, ch. 10, and *Shih chi*, ch. 40. Kuo P'u (276–324) and P'ei Yin (5th cen.) wrote commentaries on these two texts respectively.

54. A famous poet of the ancient Ch'u kingdom who flourished in the 3d century B.C.

ful, far superior to those at Tzu-kuei, but the town is unimaginably bleak and desolate. There are hardly more than a hundred houses, and from the magistrate's office on down, every building has a thatched roof—there's not a trace of tile. Wang K'ang-nien, who is temporarily acting in lieu of a magistrate, and Tu Te-hsien, who serves as both secretary and military commander, came to call. Both are men of Shu.

I paid my respects at the shrine of Lord K'ou Lai [55] and climbed the Autumn Wind Pavilion, gazing down at the river and mountains. The day was dark and overcast and fine snow whirled and tumbled through the air—all this, plus the name of the pavilion, was enough to make me feel quite downcast, and for the first time I sighed like a man banished to the far corners of the sky.

Later I climbed Twin Cypress Hall and White Cloud Pavilion. In old times there were cypresses in front of the hall planted by Lord K'ou Lai, but now they have all withered and died. The heaped up mountains to the south, however, are tall and striking—a delight to look at. As for White Cloud Pavilion, it is one of the rarest and most beautiful spots in the world. Crowds of mountains ring and enfold it, its upper stories now and then rising into sight above them; old trees grow dark around it, some of them two or three hundred years old. Beyond the railing a pair of waterfalls pour down into the rocky stream bed, scattering pearls, raining down beads of jade, with a cold that pierces the bone. Below this point, the stream becomes the River of Mercy, racing and tumbling on to join the Yangtze. Since I left Wu and came to Ch'u, I have

55. K'ou Chun (961–1023), a prominent statesman of Northern Sung times. In his youth he served as magistrate of Pa-tung District and that is presumably why there was a shrine to him there.

traveled more than five thousand li and have passed through fifteen provinces, but I have never seen a pavilion or tower to match White Cloud. What's more, it is situated right behind the district offices. Pa-tung is a place where nothing ever happens, and anyone who became its magistrate would be able to eat and sleep in the pavilion and enjoy endless delight. And yet the post of magistrate has been vacant now for two or three years and no one is willing to accept the assignment. Why is that?

22d day: We set out from Pa-tung. The mountains are increasingly wonderful and strange in shape. We saw something called the Grotto of the Master, an opening high up on the face of the sheer cliff. I can't imagine how anyone could climb up to such a place, yet it looks as though there's a railing around it. Who the "Master" is, I don't know.

We passed Three Branch Spring, which flows out of a hole in the mountain, but it had only two branches. Popular lore says that if the spring has three branches, it will be a year of plenty; if two branches, a middling harvest; if one branch or no flow at all, a famine. We tied up at Weary Rock. At night it rained.

23d day: We passed the Taoist Temple of Concentrated Truth on Shaman Mountain. I paid my respects at the Shrine of the Immortal of Wondrous Works, popularly known as the Goddess of Shaman Mountain.[56] The shrine faces directly to-

56. Peach Princess, daughter of the Red Emperor, the god of the south. She was made famous by a poem, the "*Fu* on Kao-t'ang" by Sung Yü (see p. 115, n. 53), which tells how the goddess visited King Huai of Ch'u (r. 328–229 B.C.) in a dream and slept with him. When she took her leave, she said "at dawn I am the morning clouds, at evening I am the passing rain," a pronouncement repeatedly alluded to in Chinese amorous poetry.

ward Shaman Mountain, whose peaks soar upward to the sky and whose feet stick straight out into the river. Authorities on such matters say that neither Mount T'ai or Mount Hua, Mount Heng or Mount Lu can match its wonders. Of its twelve peaks, however, not all are visible. Among the eight or nine which one can see, the goddess's peak is the most slender and superb of all, a fitting place for an immortal to dwell. The priest of the shrine says that each year on the fifteenth day of the eighth month, when the moon is full, the sound of flutes and strings can be heard echoing back and forth on the peak. The mountain monkeys all begin to wail, and only at dawn does the sound gradually fade away. Halfway up the mountain behind the shrine is a stone platform, level and broad. According to legend, Emperor Yü of the Hsia called upon the goddess and she presented him with a written charm on this platform.[57] Seen from here, the twelve peaks look like so many screens. Today the weather was perfectly clear, without a trace of cloud or mist in any of the four directions. Only above the goddess's peak were there a few wisps of white cloud, like cranes or *luan* birds soaring and dancing, lingering on and on and never scattering—it was most uncanny. In old times there were several hundred crows at the shrine which came out to greet the boats of travelers and send them off. Already in a poem by Li Yi, a governor of K'uei-chou in T'ang times, we find the line: "Flocks of crows feast on leftovers from the sacrifice." [58] But recently, in the first year of the *ch'ien-tao* era (1165), they suddenly ceased to appear and now

57. On Emperor Yü of the Hsia, see p. 110, n. 48.

58. Probably meant to be Li Yi-sun, governor of K'uei-chou in the *cheng-yüan* era (785–804). I can find no extant poetry by him, but two brief prose pieces are preserved in *Ch'üan T'ang wen* ch. 544, one a description of the sights of K'uei-chou.

there is not a single crow. I don't know the reason for this.

We tied up at Clear Water Grotto. The grotto is very deep and has a rear opening that comes out on the other side of the mountain. But it is pitch black, with water running down the middle, so very few people attempt to enter it. Prayers for rain offered here in time of drought are very likely to be answered.

24th day: In the morning we reached Shaman Mountain District. It is in a gorge and very impressive—the town is superior to Kuei-chou or Hsia-chou. On the other side of the river is Nan-ling, a large, tall mountain with a road like a thread winding back and forth to the summit. It is called the Hundred and Eight Bends and is the main road to Shih-chou.

In the district office is an old iron basin with a pointed bottom, like half a water jar. It is thick and sturdy and inside has an inscription which says it was made in the *yung-p'ing* era of the Han (58–75). Where it is nicked, the iron glows with a black color like fine lacquer. The characters are bold and simple in style and it is altogether an admirable piece.

I visited the old detached palace of the kingdom of Ch'u, popularly called the Palace of Slim Waists. There is a lake which in ancient times was the scene of banquets and entertainments, but now it is silted up and has almost disappeared. On three sides the mountains are all bare, but the river and the mountains to the south present a splendid sight. There is also a grave of a general of the Eastern Chin period (317–419). A stone stele stands beside the grave, but the base has sunk into the ground and the stone leans forward as though it were about to fall. Barely half the characters are legible.

25th day: Late in the afternoon we reached Big Valley Mouth and tied up the boat. The region produces beautiful pears the size of measuring cups.

26th day: We set out from Big Valley Mouth and entered Ch'ü-t'ang Gorge. The two sides of the gorge soar up into the sky, their faces as smooth as though they had been cut with a knife. Overhead, the sky looks like a strip of glossy silk. The water has fallen and even in the gorge is as smooth as oil in a cruet. We passed Holy Matron Spring. It is situated in a cleft on the top of the rock. If a person stands beside it and gives a loud shout, the water spurts out, and if he gives a number of shouts, it spurts out a number of times—very strange.

In the evening we reached Ch'ü-t'ang Pass. The west gate of the pass faces directly toward the Yen-yü-tui, a pile of broken rocks that sticks up thirty or forty chang out of the water. The local people say that in summer and fall, when the river is at its highest, the water in turn rises thirty or forty chang above the top of the pile. I went through the pass by sedan chair and paid my respects at the Shrine of the White Emperor. It has an air of great antiquity, with pines and cypresses all several hundred years old. There are several inscribed stone stelae, all erected in the time of the Posterior Shu (934–965). In the garden is an ornamental stone shaped like a bamboo shoot inscribed with the words "Huang Lu-chih, *chien-chung ching-kuo* first year (1101)." [59] There is also the Hall of the Duke of Yüeh, built by Yang Su during the Sui dynasty (581–617), which Tu Fu has described in a poem.[60] The original building

59. Huang T'ing-chien (1045–1105), the famous Northern Sung poet and disciple of Su Tung-p'o.

60. Yang Su (d. 606) was a prominent statesman of the Sui; he was enfeoffed with the title of Duke of Yüeh. Tu Fu's poem, entitled "Written when I joined the other gentlemen to climb up the tower of White Emperor City and dine at the Hall of the Duke of Yüeh," was written in 766, when he had just arrived in the K'uei-chou and White Emperor area. In the fall of the following year, he lived for a time at East Village.

fell into ruin long ago; the present one was built in recent years and is large and imposing. From the pass east is called East Village, the place where Tu Fu once lived.

27th day: Early in the morning we reached K'uei-chou. The city is built on the sand at the foot of the mountains. Compared to White Emperor, it is rather flat and open, but it lacks the steepness appropriate to a pass and has no other natural features to distinguish it. It is west of the Nang River and therefore is also called Nang West. People hereabouts tell me that a river which flows out of the mountains and into the Yangtze is called a *nang*. Southeast of the city are the so-called Rocks of the Eight Tactics laid out by Chu-ko Liang, broken stones laid out in rows as though with a measuring line.[61] Each year when the river rises, the rocks are covered by thirty or forty chang of water, but when it recedes, the rows of rocks are just as before.

61. The rows of rocks supposedly represented eight tactical formations for troops in battle invented by Chu-ko Liang (181–234), the famous statesman and general of the state of Shu in the Three Kingdoms period.

Translations From The Oriental Classics

The Complete Works of Chuang Tzu, tr. Burton Watson 1968

The Romance of the Western Chamber (Hsi Hsiang chi) tr. S. I. Hsiung 1968

The Manyōshū, Nippon Gakujutsu Shinkōkai edition. Paperback text edition. 1969

Records of the Historian: Chapters from the Shih chi of Ssu-ma Ch'ien. Paperback text edition, tr. Burton Watson 1969

Cold Mountain: 100 Poems by the T'ang Poet Han-shan, tr. Burton Watson. Also in paperback ed. 1970

Twenty Plays of the Nō Theatre, ed. Donald Keene. Also in paperback ed. 1970

Chūshingura: The Treasury of Loyal Retainers, tr. Donald Keene 1971

The Zen Master Hakuin: Selected Writings, tr. Philip B. Yampolsky 1971

Chinese Rhyme-Prose, tr. Burton Watson 1971

Kūkai: Major Works, tr. Yoshito S. Hakeda 1972

The Old Man Who Does as He Pleases: Selections from the Poetry and Prose of Lu Yu, tr. Burton Watson 1973

The Lion's Roar of Queen Śrīmālā, tr. Alex & Hideko Wayman 1974

Studies In Oriental Culture

Companions To Asian Studies

Introduction To Oriental Civilizations

Wm. Theodore de Bary, *Editor*